NDE:

near death experience

and AWARE studies

proof of the soul

and God?

UPDATED
2025

ORSON WEDGWOOD

Published by Orson Wedgwood.

ISBN: 978-1-8383631-1-6

Cover design & interior formatting:
Mark Thomas / Coverness.com

ACKNOWLEDGEMENTS

I would like to thank Susan Hughes and Lisa Stilwell for editing this book. I would like to thank Christine Short for proof-reading and I would like to thank Mark Thomas for the cover and interior design. I would also like to thank all the regular contributors from my blog on NDEs, awareofaware.com, who have shared my interest and helped me develop my understanding of this subject. In particular I would like to thank "Z" who provided some editorial comments, and the other top 10 contributors over the years: Tim, David, Eduardo, Samwise, Bippy123, Alan, RegenKingRepris, Lukas, Max_B, Mery and our resident skeptic - Chad. Most of all I would like to thank my wife, Kirsty, who along with providing excellent editorial and developmental support, has encouraged me at every step of the way to persevere with this project that we both believe is of great importance.

TABLE OF CONTENTS

FOREWORD

This updated version includes the latest data from AWARE II published in Summer 2023. We now have sufficient evidence to declare what the truth is regarding the validity, or otherwise, of NDEs, and by inference, whether or not the soul may be eternal, whether there is a heaven, whether there is a hell, and whether or not God exists.

However, there is something else, something of urgent importance that has been largely glossed over by the NDE literature to this point which created a moral imperative for this book to be written. There is a finding from NDE research that is so central to all of humanity's well being that to not address it would be unconscionable. This sense of urgency was heightened on release of a recent book by one of the most respected authors and researchers on the subject, Bruce Greyson. *After*, published in March 2021, is a great read, and covers a wealth of fascinating material from the career of a man who has dedicated his life to improving our collective understanding of NDEs. Despite this, he doesn't fully address the subject of why only a minority of people who are brought back from clinical death report NDEs.

Since NDEs are now proven beyond reasonable doubt to be real, the question of why reports of NDEs decline so precipitously with age becomes the single most important question to ask, and the answers may not be as obvious as many, including Bruce Greyson, have previously stated. The data clearly shows that changes in memory function with age alone cannot account for this huge difference, even when combined with other possible causes.

After examining the overall evidence for and against NDEs, what happens to those who have them, including where they go and who they meet, this book assesses the different potential explanations for why it might be that not everyone reports an NDE, and why the implications could be of fundamental importance to all humanity. Many will find one of these possible explanations deeply unsettling, but if it is true, then it may be the single most significant truth that we can learn in this life. That is no exaggeration. Understanding this truth, and what might lie behind it, may be the difference between opening the door to a future of infinite wonder versus experiencing a lost eternity or even Hell. The fact that a significant proportion of NDErs report Hell-like experiences is one aspect of this subject that is often ignored or dismissed.

That is why this book may be one of the most important you ever read. Therefore it is worth persevering with the detailed sections about the background and the studies, because they form the foundations of scientific knowledge and rational thinking that this vital truth is built on.

INTRODUCTION

SCIENCE MAY SAVE YOUR SOUL

Morgan Freeman: "Is there any scientific support for the idea of the soul?"

Dr. Sam Parnia: "Today we call the soul consciousness in science. So, we can test this theory scientifically and see—does consciousness continue or does it stop. The evidence we have is that when a person dies ...the soul—the consciousness—doesn't become annihilated ...at least in the early period of death."

Above is an excerpt from an interview that Morgan Freeman conducted with Dr. Sam Parnia, MD, in New York as part of Freeman's 2016 TV series called "The Story of God."[1] Just contemplate for a moment the words *when a person*

---

1   The Story of God with Morgan Freeman, produced by the National Geographic Channel and released in April 2016. Now available on Netflix.

dies, the soul doesn't become annihilated. These words, if supported by the evidence, turn the modern world upside down and they are what NDEs and the AWARE studies are about.

Dr. Sam Parnia is associate professor of Medicine at New York University (NYU) Langone Medical Center and a leading researcher in resuscitation medicine. Much of his work has been spent in British and American emergency rooms using modern medical techniques to literally bring people back from the dead, or in medical terms, achieve return of spontaneous circulation (ROSC). Some of his research focuses on improving these techniques so that when people do achieve ROSC, they do not suffer brain damage and can function as they did before. While I consider this work important and noble, it is not what this book is about.

Dr. Parnia is better known for his research into a phenomenon that he and many other ER health care professionals (HCPs) have encountered over the years: near-death experiences (NDEs). Dr. Parnia has conducted two international multi-center clinical studies—AWARE I and AWARE II—in hospitals across the world under the AWARE (AWAreness during REsuscitation) study umbrella. I believe these are the most important clinical studies ever undertaken, and that everyone should know about them and the conclusions that can be drawn. My career as a medical scientist has focused on clinical research, so I am conscious of how bold a statement that is, especially when you consider all the life extending studies showing improvement in the treatment of heart disease, cancer, and HIV, etc. Let me explain why I make it.

Consider this question: What is most important to you in life?

To some, it might be their children or a spouse; for others, happiness, success, or a long, healthy life. Still others might say their faith is the most important thing because it leads to eternal life.

I, along with many billions of people, have long believed in the existence of the eternal soul, which has no natural explanation. Based on this belief, I decided long ago it was probably smart to look after my soul and prioritize its well-being beyond death. However, until now, this belief was an act of faith based on subjective understanding. There are many people who believe that everything, including consciousness, has a natural explanation and that there is no such thing as an eternal soul. They also form this belief based on equally subjective interpretations of information relating to this subject. This is the materialist world view[2]. Prior to this point in history, there have not been any objectively proven facts that shed light on which of these opposing beliefs about the nature and origins of consciousness is true. Has that changed?

What if the evidence proves beyond reasonable doubt that the soul is indeed an entity that is able to exist beyond death, potentially for eternity? Wouldn't that impact how people answer the question of what is most important in life? Wouldn't it in fact change the way everyone throughout the world behaves?

If you already believe we have an eternal soul, this book might solidify that belief and increase your determination to look after your soul. It might also encourage you to share your knowledge with others out of concern for their souls. But what if you are one of the countless millions who have dismissed the idea of a soul and eternity as superstitious nonsense. Or maybe you are someone who has not given this much thought until now. Would your view of life and your opinion of what is most important change if you were provided proof that your consciousness (which will also be referred to as your "soul" throughout this book) has the capacity to live beyond the death of your physical body?

Materialism, which has been the cause of most of humanity's current problems, has reigned in much of the world in different forms for at least a century. In the West it is most obvious in unbridled capitalism; in Russia

---

2 Materialism, in the context of philosophy is similar to atheism, although atheism is specific to belief that there is no God. I use both to mean the same thing in this book - a belief that there is nothing beyond the observed natural order.

and China during the last century, in socialism; in many developing countries, as state-sanctioned cronyism or oligarchism. Material objectives prevail under all these systems, whether the goal be individual (capitalist) or collective (socialist) material improvement. Never is the well-being of the soul considered to be a priority when governments set new policy or when academics create new curricula. In many instances belief systems that focus on the spiritual aspect of life are actively opposed or dismissed by establishment materialist orders.

If the results of the AWARE studies show, or prove, beyond reasonable doubt that the soul survives death, then they have the potential to transform societies and shift humanity's focus away from purely material objectives. If we learned that we are indeed much more than a collection of molecules with one short existence, wouldn't our thinking adapt toward a different approach to life? If our consciousness—our "selves"—could potentially live forever, wouldn't our absolute priority become ensuring the health and survival of our soul?

That is why I state that clinical studies seeking to find ways to extend life by a few years would pale into insignificance compared to studies demonstrating that eternal life of the soul is a possibility.

But there is more …

If the evidence shows that consciousness survives death, they also potentially prove by rational extrapolation of NDE reports that God exists. In addition, they open the door to learning what happens to the soul after the body has died, and of fundamental importance whether all souls survive death, or just some, and whether a heaven and/or a hell exist. These aspects will be discussed in more detail later in this book along with emerging evidence that the longer we live, the lower the chance that our consciousness persists beyond the end of physical life.

I hope you enjoy coming with me on this journey of scientific and philosophical discovery. My goal is to share my understanding of what near death experiences and out of body experiences (OBEs) are; how the AWARE studies were designed; what results they produced; what other evidence exists which shows beyond doubt these experiences are real; and finally, to explore answers to the "so what?" question. I will also share some initial thoughts on the basics of looking after your soul, without getting into the specifics of my own faith—that can be found in my book *NDE: Did Jesus Die For Nothing? The evidence from NDEs.* I want everyone to be able to benefit from this book and gain insight into what is not only a fascinating subject, but one that is of central importance.

Having said this, while I will try to be as objective as possible, complete objectivity is impossible for anyone, so please do fact-check anything that challenges your current understanding. Rather than dismiss a claim, I hope you will dig deeper on your own. It is important that you keep an open mind, lay aside preconceptions and consider all new data or theories as objectively as you can. After all, it may well be that the destiny of your eternal soul depends on it.

CHAPTER 1

NDES AND OBES: NEAR DEATH, DURING DEATH, AFTER DEATH, NEVER DEAD?

Before we can take our first step on this journey of understanding, we must know where we are going. To determine that we must ask the question: "What is a near death experience?" The term signifies an experience when someone is near death or appears to actually be dead. However, there is a lot of debate among scientists and clinicians about exactly when this occurs. Some believe it to happen while a person is clinically dead; others think it occurs before clinical death, or during the few seconds after the heart stops and while the brain is in the process of shutting down but is briefly still capable of consciousness.

In his book, *The Lazarus Effect,* Dr. Sam Parnia refers to NDEs as "actual death experiences" (ADEs).[3] He argues that the term "near death" is

---

3   There have been two subsequent revisions to the convention of naming these experiences, the most recent of which is to call them REDs - Recalled Experience of Death. I discuss this later.

misleading since, according to medical criteria, those who experience NDEs are clinically dead, not near death. They then return to life from clinical death once they are revived—they achieve ROSC.

So what is death? Death is arguably the absence of life. What is life, or more specifically, what constitutes a living human being?

To be alive, your blood must be circulating at sufficient levels to provide oxygenated blood to your vital organs, and at the same time, remove blood containing waste products such as carbon dioxide which is exhaled or toxins that are filtered by your kidneys and excreted in your urine, or metabolized by the liver. Once blood flow falls below critical levels, organs stop functioning, toxic substances start accumulating, and the cells that constitute your body are damaged beyond repair. Especially relevant to this book and the AWARE studies is the fact that, within seconds of stopped blood flow, the brain is no longer capable of conscious activity.

Consciousness—thought, self-awareness, observations, and so on—is a higher function of the brain demanding large amounts of chemical energy and oxygen. When these processes occur, there is a lot of activity on what is called an electroencephalogram—an electronic brain monitor—or an EEG. The same is true of dreams, which are just a different state of consciousness. In either instance, for such consciousness to occur, the brain and heart need to function at normal or near normal levels.

The standard definition of the word 'death' is the irreversible state in which a person has no heartbeat or conscious activity. Note the use of the word irreversible. Death is normally defined as a permanent state. Clinical death is the one exception to this rule, and is a state in which again, there is no heartbeat or brain activity, but the person could either recover spontaneously, or through medical intervention. In the absence of specialist equipment, either form of death is determined by the lack of a pulse and the pupil's lack of response to light. In modern hospitals it is when both the ECG (electrocardiograph or heart monitor) and the EEG are flatlining.

Before the advent of modern resuscitation techniques in the 1950s, most people who had a cardiac arrest (CA) were indeed "dead." But sometimes a person who appeared dead would come back to life, which is why in Victorian times, people were sometimes buried with a bell in their coffin so they could ring it and be "saved by the bell." However, it is unlikely their hearts had stopped and then restarted unaided. It is more likely they entered some sort of "death-like" coma with minimal respiration or detectable heartbeat.

Although Dr. Parnia and other ER HCPs prefer to define death as the cessation of heart and brain activity, they also acknowledge that there is a difference between this clinical definition of immediate death—which is reversible if ROSC occurs very soon afterwards—and irreversible or permanent death, which in the absence of major organ damage can be a process that takes hours to complete.

Cellular death is the key factor in permanent death. Once a certain number of cells have died, it is no longer possible to bring a viable body back to life. This point was once usually considered to be a few minutes after the heart and brain had stopped functioning. Now, through some of the modern resuscitation techniques pioneered by Dr. Parnia and other clinical researchers, the point at which permanent death occurs can be delayed for much longer.

One technique is to cool the body in order to slow down cell death. A notorious piece of research published in April 2019 shows the potential viability of cells in pig brains for hours after the pigs had been killed.[4] This points to the possibility of people being revived hours after death with much of their brain tissue remaining undamaged. Indeed, there have been several instances where people have fallen into extremely cold water and, after being clinically dead for ten minutes or longer, they were resuscitated and able to stage a full recovery. A particularly well-known example of this is when a

---

4   Nature 568, 283–284 (2019)

boat capsized in a lake in Denmark in 2011, and seven children were thrown into the icy water. All of them were clinically dead with no heartbeat for six hours, but through careful, slow warming, all seven eventually achieved ROSC with no permanent brain damage. Another well documented example is of Anna Bågenholm, who in 2000, fell through a frozen-over lake and remained under water for forty minutes before her body was recovered.[5] After receiving resuscitation, she, too, eventually achieved ROSC. Anna was clinically dead with no heartbeat or blood flow to the brain, but due to the sudden cooling of the body, the process of cellular decay was slowed, which allowed a viable recovery. She was dead but not permanently dead.

Skeptical scientists and physicians who do not believe the validity of NDEs or that the consciousness is a separate entity that is able to survive physical death, argue that any person who can be revived after CA has the potential for consciousness or some level of brain function between the time the heart stops and ROSC. The argument is that the brain is still functional, therefore it could have functioned. In general, this is shown not to be the case by the universal observation that consciousness is associated with strong and distinct EEG activity. The fact is that when the heart stops beating, noteworthy EEG activity of this kind stops within a few seconds. Believing that a brain can produce consciousness when there is no supply of oxygenated blood is like believing a computer without a source of power can perform the function of processing. Both are impossible. A brain without blood supply may stay *functional* for a period, but without blood flow, it cannot function.

The only exceptions of consciousness in the absence of heartbeat in humans are when an artificial supply of oxygenated blood is provided at sufficiently high levels to allow higher level brain function. There have been rare instances when advanced CPR has been administered and the patient

5   Gilbert, Mads; Gilbert M; Busund R; Skagseth A; Nilsen P; Solbo J (2000). "Resuscitation from accidental hypothermia of 13.7°C with circulatory arrest". The Lancet. 355 (9201): 375–376. doi:10.1016/S0140-6736(00)01021-7

has had passing conscious episodes despite having no pulse.[6] This is due to the high quality of the resuscitation being administered, which produces sufficient blood flow to allow the brain to function at near normal levels. Dr. Parnia addresses this potential issue through the excellent design of AWARE II where experiences can be directly correlated with EEG and ECG activity.

While reports of momentary consciousness during CPR in the absence of a heartbeat are very rare, they do provide skeptics with a potentially plausible explanation as to why people may have conscious episodes and form memories such as those described in NDEs. However, even if that explanation were true for some elements of an NDE, it does not and cannot explain validated OBEs—an issue I will discuss in more detail very shortly. In summary, there is no natural explanation, whether it be drugs, undetected brain activity during CPR, or any other physiological phenomenon, that can account for a fully validated OBE. This central fact lies at the heart of our discussions and therefore if validated OBEs exist we have conclusive proof that the consciousness is a separate entity from the brain and can survive death.

Now that we have differentiated between the states of being alive, clinical death, [permanent] death, and why neither of the latter can support consciousness, assume that when I use the term NDE in the pages ahead, I'll be referring to experiences that began while the subject had a flatline ECG and EEG, signaling the absence of heart and brain activity and therefore was in a state of clinical death.

Thousands of patients over the years claim to have experienced consciousness in the form of NDEs while their hearts and brains were not functioning. These people sometimes describe visual and/or auditory recollections of specific events occurring around them, or people near them, or even names of medications used—all details they should not have

---

6   Can Fam Physician. 2018 Jul; 64(7): 514–517

been aware of if they were truly unconscious. In about 25 percent of cases, NDErs (people who have an NDE) reported making these observations from outside of their bodies, hence the term "out of body experience" or OBE. They often describe feeling no emotional attachment toward their body nor did they feel panic. They are best described as being dispassionate about the events unfolding, as though they are neutral observers. There are exceptions of course, but this is a common theme.

As mentioned, many NDErs are credible citizens, as are the doctors and health care workers who recorded their testimonials. Many doctors and nurses in ER rooms have their own set of NDE stories that defy natural explanation. This was in fact how Sam Parnia came to be interested in the subject.

I also became interested after two people described NDEs to me. One was a woman I briefly dated who told me how she had an asthma attack while hiking in Peru. She popped out of her body and saw her friends try to resuscitate her. She also saw two of her friends kiss outside of the tent her body was in, something that was later verified.

The other NDE I heard of was experienced by someone closer to me—my father. When he was a young boy he was cycling and got knocked down by a car. Suddenly he found himself hovering above his body while people tried to revive him—a classic example of an OBE. There is one thing I'm certain of: my father didn't lie.

An OBE is one of the core elements of an NDE, and since it is the only one that can be validated using scientific technique, it is a vital piece of evidence to collect and measure. Scientifically proving that an OBE occurred would verify that NDEs are real, which would, in turn, prove that the soul lives beyond death and is an entity separate from the body.

Why would a scientifically validated OBE establish that the soul lives beyond death? If the brain and heart have stopped working, the eyes are closed, and the visual and auditory nerves are inactive—it is completely impossible for the brain to observe or record visual or auditory stimuli. There is no natural scientific explanation for how they could physically observe or record anything.

If reports of OBEs are scientifically verified, there is only one viable explanation: the consciousness is operating and making observations independently of the body after the body's death. How this consciousness can "see" without the use of eyes or "hear" without the use of ears is an intriguing thought. I believe that the physiological practicalities of hearing and seeing are of less importance than the philosophical points about the nature of how we observe the universe and what the universe is. Other than hints from the field of quantum mechanics, these points are entirely a matter of speculation relating to whether the universe is a physical construct at all and arguably belong in fantasy films such as *The Matrix* or arcane books on philosophy. How memory of these experiences get recorded in the brain without the brain functioning is another related and important question that will be discussed later.

While the issue of whether or not what we see and hear is "real" may be an unsettling and somewhat intellectual topic, it is an important fundamental paradox lying at the heart of the NDE and OBE phenomena. It's worth getting some kind of handle on it before we go further so as to avoid any sense of inconsistency in the conclusions that can be drawn from the results of the AWARE studies.

From a materialist scientific understanding, consciousness needs the brain to hear—this process is well understood. Sensors in our ears pick up sound waves that are translated into electrical signals, which are sent along nerves that lead to your brain. These electrical signals are then translated into the conscious understanding of that sound. Hearing is so automatic and intuitive that we do not think about how it occurs, we just hear. We are not aware of the fact that our consciousness hears nothing without the brain interpreting electronic nerve signals. This leads to an obvious question: If consciousness survives death, and in life it needs the brain to hear, surely it could not hear once the brain is dead or inactive. Or could it? This is the paradox at the center of the whole NDE/OBE phenomenon. By citing that the brain is inactive—therefore incapable of hearing or seeing—we are ignoring the apparent need of the consciousness to have a functioning brain to hear, see and record a memory of what is seen and heard!!

It is a mind-bending paradox, but that fact doesn't invalidate the veracity of NDEs or OBEs, it just demands explanations about the nature of existence that lie beyond materialistic understanding and which we are unable to prove. Therefore, it may be true that consciousness, once free of the body, is able to *observe* physical reality without the need for the physical equipment used by the same consciousness to *experience* physical reality while alive. In other words, when we are physically alive our consciousness experiences the physical world using physical equipment in our bodies, but once we are physically dead, the same consciousness is still able to observe the physical world only without the use of physical equipment. In one state we are participants; in the other, observers.

That can be the only explanation for how people see and hear during OBEs if they are proven real.

This raises numerous questions about the physical world, and the answers can only be theoretical and philosophical in nature. They are completely untestable, but at the same time, they lead us to ponder the nature of the experienced physical "reality" which we are accustomed to. It is a question related to the meaning of life and one that I will return to later. For now, though, if it is proven through scientific experiments, such as the AWARE studies, that consciousness is able to survive independently of the brain and body, then the paradox, while unsettling, is also proven true. I will explore this further in the Appendix.

*

To proceed without getting bogged down, we must accept that a verified OBE can only be explained by allowing for a consciousness that has the potential to observe and record memories of events while independent of the body and the brain. Dr. Parnia has previously asserted that according to scientific evidence, for at least a short time after death, the soul, or consciousness, is indeed able to persist without the "host" body. This is hugely controversial to a scientific community that works under the informal dogma of methodological materialism—meaning there is always a natural explanation for everything. As a result, there is significant and powerful opposition to formal research into NDEs from within the academic establishment.

Since the emergence of the theory of evolution, which cemented the modern foundation of science in materialism, many scientists have assumed that consciousness is something produced by the brain. No one has ever been able to explain how, but it is postulated that our sense of being—our ability to interpret our senses and communicate with the world around us—is a result of the brain's activity. The understanding that NDEs, and specifically OBEs, are evidence that the consciousness can exist independently of a functioning brain, contradicts this materialistic understanding. Specifically, it points to the brain and the rest of your body as being just a "host" or "receptacle" of your consciousness or soul, rather than the generator of it.

It is widely understood that the scientific community is disproportionately represented by atheists compared to those from other disciplines. Moreover, those who do have faith are wary about speaking out about their beliefs since doing so can have career-limiting effects. In an email I received from Dr. Parnia, he alluded to the significant opposition that he had experienced in setting up his studies. Scientists, like all humans, are tribal. The scientific tribe has become one of the most powerful tribes on earth as it holds the keys to knowledge that is central to modern living. Because many members of this tribe have publicly adopted an atheist stance and built their credibility around this position, they feel threatened when challenged with evidence that undermines their central materialistic belief. When people are threatened, they do not always respond fairly or even rationally, and such has been the case with some scientists in their treatment of any viable research that doesn't support their materialistic atheist position.

If the OBE was proven to be real, it would provide evidence consistent with religious belief and completely shatter the current central dogma of science—materialism—that has been in place since the 1800s.

Well, this being said, I believe the horse has bolted and the evidence we have upends the dogma of materialism forever. Let's see why.

CHAPTER 2

REPORTING AND RESEARCH OF NDES

THE FOUNDING OF THE FIELD—PRE-1980

Now we can really start out on the journey, and we will be walking in the footsteps of the pioneers of the field.

Near death experiences have reportedly occurred throughout history, even going back to antiquity.[7] The first medical report was by a French military doctor in 1740.[8] However, before the advent of modern CPR in the 1950s, spontaneous revival was not common. If you had a heart attack and your heart stopped, you were considered permanently dead, and the opportunity to experience an NDE was extremely limited. As a result, reports

---

7   https://digital.library.unt.edu/ark:/67531/metadc461731/

8   https://www.livescience.com/46993-oldest-medical-report-of-near-death-experience.html

of NDEs were rare, and NDEs were not fully understood for what they were; people didn't necessarily understand that someone had actually died and come back to life. In our modern era, people dying and being revived with CPR happens every day in many of the hundreds of thousands of hospitals across the world. If the NDE is a real phenomenon, one would expect to hear about them occurring more frequently throughout the past six decades—and this is precisely what has happened, especially in North America and Europe.

Initially, however, such reports by patients were dismissed by physicians and nurses as hallucinations, or even as evidence of psychiatric disorders. Given the skeptical response from health professionals in industrialized countries, many of the early NDErs kept quiet about their experiences, only disclosing them when the public, and some in the medical profession, became more accepting. The perception of NDEs began changing after the 1975 publication of Raymond Moody's book *Life After Life*. Moody, a clinical psychologist who had listened to patients' reports about NDEs for a number of years, decided that the phenomenon was most likely real. His book, which recounted many of the experiences, caused a media storm, and interest has only grown since.

There were a number of subsequent books by other leaders in the field, such as psychologist Ken Ring, who published *Life at Death* in 1980, and Dr. Michael Sabbom, who published *Recollections of Death: A Medical Investigation* in 1984. A cardiologist and professor of medicine, Dr. Sabbom was the first physician to publish on this topic, bringing it even more attention. Bruce Greyson was another founding father of research into NDEs, and in 1984 he co-authored the book *The Near-Death Experience: Problems, Prospects, Perspectives*.

This initial flurry of activity was followed by years of more books of subjective accounts confirmed by health care professionals. Some included OBE reports in which patients reported seeing objects in neighboring rooms and even on ledges outside the hospital while clinically dead—reports that were later verified independently.

One of the more famous NDEs that has been discussed over the years is that of Pam Reynolds, a well-known record producer in the eighties and nineties. She had a brain aneurysm in 1991 and was deliberately brought into a state of near death so doctors could operate and stop the leaking in her brain. During the operation she had ear buds taped into her ears that played a very loud sound so that the doctors could record any EEG activity and know when to increase sedation.

Pam Reynolds described "popping" outside of her head. For a while she said she remained in the room, hovering above her body. She observed the number of people in the room, the instruments being used, and a discussion around which artery to use for a procedure. She also reported meeting a dead relative and then being pushed back into her broken body. After the operation she told the neurosurgeon what she had seen, and he confirmed all the details. He was as convinced as she was that she had an NDE with OBE since he believed it was impossible for her to have seen or heard anything. This is a typical "anecdotal" account, albeit reported by a well-known figure and verified by a respected medical professional.

The details of the common core elements of NDEs started to become better characterized and eventually formalized in the Greyson NDE scale, which I will discuss in more detail below. Books and TV shows sensationalizing NDEs were all the rage in the 1980s and early 1990s. But as time went by, the reluctance of the medical and academic establishment to give it serious thought, and the endless insistence by materialist scientists who believed that NDEs were produced by the brain, meant that those who believed in NDEs were categorized with those who believe in astrology. Thousands of reports by credible witnesses, including pilots, lawyers, engineers, servicemen, teachers, and university professors, along with verifications from reliable attending medical professionals, meant absolutely nothing to the hardened skeptics.

However, not all the blame for disbelief lies with materialist skeptics—

the NDE community itself must also be blamed. Dozens of NDE websites and societies, some of which were once balanced and reliable, began to embrace the excesses of the New Age movement and espouse concepts alien to Western thinking, and they were eventually regarded as somewhat bizarre. Some of these New Age inferences are also not necessarily correlated with the NDE reports of the early researchers. Proponents of the New Age movement might explain that this is because the vast majority of early work was conducted in the West, and mostly in the USA, which is predominantly Christian. Either way, it is fair to say that the NDE community has attracted more than its fair share of unhinged attention seekers. As well, many of these websites encourage people to add their own NDEs, and while this may attract a large number of genuine reports, any such accounts leave them open to the obvious accusation of not being remotely objective, or of describing experiences that fall outside of the classical definition of an NDE.

For scientists like myself and others, this is very off-putting and gives plenty of ammunition to the materialist skeptics. Thankfully, some serious and highly qualified medical researchers shared a genuine curiosity about the subject and, in the late 1980s, began to conduct more rigorous academic clinical research. They realized that anecdotal accounts like those of Pam Reynolds were not going to be enough to convince the skeptics, so they set about designing studies that would investigate the phenomenon by using the scientific method. This consisted of systematic observation, measurement, and experiment, alongside the formulation, testing, and modification of hypotheses. A hypothesis is a supposition or proposed explanation made on the basis of limited evidence as a starting point for further investigation.[9] Simply put, a hypothesis is a statement that potentially explains an observed phenomenon and the scientific method is the process by which the statement is determined true or not and is summarized as follows:

---

9   Online Oxford dictionary.

Make observations > generate a hypothesis that explains those observations > design and conduct an experiment that tests the hypothesis > hypothesis validated > end process or show false/imperfect findings > modify original hypothesis or generate new one > design new experiment, etc.

This is the way good science is conducted, and I will come back to this later a number of times.

PUBLISHED SCIENTIFIC STUDIES—1980s AND ONWARD

At this point on our journey the road becomes a bit steeper for a while as we navigate the important clinical and scientific data that underpins our understanding of NDEs. Stick with it though, the rewards are worth the effort.

In my world, you are not taken seriously as a researcher unless you are published in a reputable scientific journal. The world's two most respected general medical journals are *The Lancet* and *The New England Journal of Medicine*. To be published in a journal such as these, you must produce research that generates advances in knowledge, such as a new hypothesis or work that disproves or provides further substantial validation of a previous hypothesis.

So, for NDEs to be considered a subject of genuine scientific enquiry rather than just an eccentric belief in a paranormal phenomenon, medical researchers need to undertake a well-designed research study and publish results that either validate or disprove the experience.

What is the nature of a research study? In a well-designed research study of any kind, a hypothesis is generated by the researcher(s), and the experiment or study is designed around proving or discounting the hypothesis. For example, after observations from early proof-of-concept studies of the effects of various drugs for controlling blood pressure, a hypothesis is generated: drug A is better at controlling blood pressure than drug B. Next, an experiment is designed to test this hypothesis. For example, x number of patients with high blood pressure take drug A, and x number of patients with high blood pressure take drug B. Most trials have a "control," which can be a placebo and is used to compare to the new drug. In this example, drug B is the control.

The last step is "powering" the study, which is ensuring there are enough patients in the study to create an observable and statistically significant effect. A statistician makes this calculation using data from previous proof-of-concept studies that give a ballpark figure of effect, and including enough subjects in the new study to ensure a 95 percent or more level of confidence that the effect is real. [10] Usually a well-designed clinical trial "randomizes" the patients. In other words, a computer randomly selects patients to go on either drug. The trial is double blinded; neither the patient nor the healthcare professional involved knows whether the patient is taking drug A or B. Furthermore, a good clinical study is "prospective" in that it is set up before patients are recruited so that there is consistency in terms of data collected, the types of patients admitted to the study, and the degree of randomization and blinding. Retrospective studies that collect data after the events occurred are much more open to bias and irregularities.

The first tranche of studies that aimed to achieve a scientific understanding and validation of NDEs were published in the early 2000s. Attempts were made to follow the scientific method, with varying degrees of success. All of the researchers were pioneers in a totally new field, therefore there was

---

10   Ninety-five percent confidence is widely used as the statistical benchmark to show that the results from the study were unlikely to have occurred by chance. Another way of putting this is that there is only a 5% or 1 in 20 chance of the results occurring by chance. This is specifically referred to as the p value, and a p of <0.05 is the gold standard.

no existing template around which to design their studies like there is with pharmaceutical studies, so mistakes were naturally made. This is how science evolves and how scientists learn.

I am now going to discuss the highlights of three important studies.

STUDY 1: NEAR-DEATH EXPERIENCE IN SURVIVORS OF CARDIAC ARREST: A PROSPECTIVE STUDY IN THE NETHERLANDS.

Pim Van Lommel, 2001. [11]

The study, published in *The Lancet*, began in 1988 and was carried out in ten hospitals in the Netherlands. Prior to this, everything presented or published had been from retrospective studies that documented accounts from patients who already had NDEs. These are open to criticism due to factors such as patient self-selection and long periods of time between the event and the interview. Van Lommel's study was the first prospective study to examine the phenomenon of NDEs in patients surviving cardiac arrest (CA). To be included in the study, the NDEs had to occur after study initiation and meet certain criteria.

In Van Lommel's study, CA survivors were interviewed within a few days of resuscitation. Follow-up interviews were conducted two years and eight years later. A number of baseline variables, such as demographic, pharmacological, physiological, and psychological factors experienced by CA patients were recorded and comparisons were made between patients who had NDEs and those who did not. NDEs were scored according to a weighted core index and determined by the presence and quality of ten core elements: awareness of being dead; positive emotions; out of body experience

11   Van Lommel, P; Lancet 2001; 358: 2039–45

(OBE); passing along a tunnel between distinct realms; communication with light; observation of colors; meeting dead people; life review; presence of border; and sense of suddenly returning to your body.

Here are highlights of the most interesting points and a discussion of the author's comments.

- A total of 18% of participants had some kind of NDE experience: 6% had a superficial NDE, 12% had a core NDE, and 7% had a deep NDE. Van Lommel suggests this may be an over-representation of true NDEs as the weighted index created false positives. In his conclusion, he suggests that the true proportion of people having NDEs is in the range of 5 to 10%. Like many other researchers, he suggests that a problem with short-term memory may account for the fact that not all survivors of CA have NDEs. This is supported by two pieces of evidence from this study:

  ◉ Age was a determining factor in patients reporting an NDE. The likelihood of reporting an NDE decreased as age increased. Short-term memory deteriorates as we age, particularly after the age of fifty, therefore it is certainly possible that the lower frequency of NDEs among older CA survivors may be due to having greater impairment of memory.

  ◉ The length of time patients underwent CPR was connected to the frequency of NDEs. Longer times reduced the number of reports. Long periods of CPR are also associated with subsequent problems with short term memory.

This study had a notable, and now famous, "veridical" OBE.[12] In the account, a nurse removed the false teeth of a subject who was in a coma after a CA, placed the teeth in a crash cart, and forgot about them. A week later, when the nurse went to visit the patient, he recognized her and told the other nurses in the room that she knew where his false teeth were. The nurse reported that he was definitely in a coma and could not have possibly seen or known what she did with his teeth or the other events he said he witnessed.

Other tidbits:

- Patients with more ROSC events had a higher chance of experiencing an NDE. For instance, if they had two CAs over a period of a year, they had a higher chance of experiencing an NDE than someone who only had one CA.
- There was no relationship between the frequency of NDEs and the time of their first interview. (The subject's memory of the NDE, once established, didn't deteriorate.)
- The interviews done two and eight years later showed that patients who had an NDE were generally more spiritual and prone to believing in an afterlife than they had been before. In contrast, patients who had not had an NDE were more likely not to believe in the afterlife and become less interested in spirituality as time progressed.

---

12   The only time I have ever come across the word *veridical* is in relation to NDEs, and it simply means "truthful." It relates to the fact that an independent witness to the events corroborated the account of the OBE. The need for this specific word is, in itself interesting, as it points to the scientific community's stance about human testimony on the matter of what they term "paranormal" events. If there were sufficient credible independent witnesses to a murder, the guilt of the accused would be regarded as fact. Despite thousands of credible witnesses to support NDEs and OBEs, the word *factual* is not countenanced.

Van Lommel notes a marked difference between the kind of experiences described by the subjects who experienced NDEs in his study compared to those who experienced NDE-like experiences induced through chemical or other means in other studies. He concludes: "NDE pushes at the limits of medical ideas about the range of human conscious and the mind brain relationship."[13]

My thoughts about this study? A low percentage of patients have NDEs. In addition, the likelihood of experiencing—or remembering an experience—deteriorates with age. Van Lommel ascribes this to deteriorating memory in older patients. However, this is a classic case of mixing association and causation. The fact that older patients are less likely to recall an NDE has two possible explanations. The first could indeed be, as the author suggests, the fact that older patients have worse memory recall, but there is another explanation: patients who grow older are less likely to have an NDE whether they remember it or not. I find it interesting, and possibly pertinent, that during the eight years after their cardiac arrests, patients who had not experienced an NDE had become progressively less interested in spirituality. This may hint at another possible but highly controversial explanation as to why percentages of patients having NDEs after resuscitation decreases with age. While most researchers on this subject suggest that they are memory related—and some of the data from this study may support that—there are other pieces of data that hint at alternative explanations. This is such an important topic, it will have its own section later.

Another interesting finding in the study is that women are more likely to experience an NDE than men, despite being older. I have often noticed that many churches have a higher proportion of women than men, and this is borne out in data from Pew Research Center's 2014 Religious Landscape

---

13   Van Lommel, P; Lancet 2001; 358: 2039–45

Study: "American women are more likely than American men to say they pray daily (64% vs. 47%) and attend religious services at least once a week (40% vs. 32%)."

I have often pondered why this might be. Might there be genetic reasons for women showing a greater predisposition toward spirituality? Historically men have been more likely than women to be involved directly in hand-to-hand violent struggle. It could be argued that the most successful would be those who are best at winning, and that to win you may be less likely to show empathy or compassion for your opponent's suffering[14]. If this psychological disposition for showing compassion is genetic, it would be more likely to be passed on to the next generation. The next generation of course has an equal chance of being male or female, so shouldn't this lack of compassion be passed on to both sexes? Maybe, but it is known that certain traits and mutations are only present on the Y chromosome, therefore only passed from father to son. This is all speculation, but in my experience, spiritual people seem more compassionate, and the finding from Van Lommel's study that women are more likely to have an NDE than men may be evidence that men are less able to remember or experience spiritual occurrences. We will venture into the poorly charted area of spirituality and genetics later.

---

14   For the sake of avoiding to appear sexually biased, I include this comment from one of my editors – "I couldn't help but raise an eyebrow here because some of the most hurtful exchanges I've had are with other women. They can be vicious!"

STUDY 2. THE INCIDENCE AND CORRELATES OF NEAR-DEATH EXPERIENCES IN A CARDIAC CARE UNIT.

Bruce Greyson, 2003; General Hospital Psychiatry.

Dr. Greyson is one of the most widely published researchers on NDEs in the established literature. He has a host of citations to his name. He is also the creator of the Greyson NDE scale, an interview tool used by researchers to establish whether the experience is an NDE or otherwise. [15] The interviewer asks twelve questions related to specific elements of NDEs. For example, one question is, "Did you have a feeling of peace or pleasantness?" The answer is then graded with a score from zero for neither, one for relief or calmness, and two for incredible peace or pleasantness. The scores are added up after all twelve questions are asked, and if the subject scores greater than seven, the experience is classified as an NDE.

This study was prospective. Subjects were included if they had been admitted to the University of Virginia Hospital with a number of possible different cardiac events, including cardiac arrest. Within six days after the patients had stabilized, they were asked to complete a questionnaire that identified various baseline, or preexisting characteristics, such as sociodemographic factors—including income and social isolation—and the severity of the cardiac incident. They were also asked to complete the Greyson scale questionnaire, and if they had a score higher than seven, they were assigned to the experiencer group.

The use of "matched controls" differentiated this study from others. Matched controls help identify what variables—changeable characteristics, such as belief—might contribute to a phenomenon when key characteristics

---

15   The Near-Death Experience Scale; Bruce Greyson, Journal of Nervous & Mental Disease 171(6):369–375 June 1983.

are fixed. In this study they "matched" the subjects who experienced NDEs with subjects who didn't but had a similar age, gender, and primary diagnosis. They identified the NDErs and the matched controls and conducted more in-depth interviews with them to establish whether or not they had prior paranormal experiences. Doing this made it possible to identify more specific factors associated with someone having an NDE. They also compared characteristics of the NDEr group to characteristics of those in the wider, unmatched, cohort who did not experience an NDE.

Here are the highlights of a few interesting findings and my comments on some of the conclusions.

- NDEs were most common in those who had survived a cardiac arrest (10%), compared to 2% of the entire cardiac event cohort many of whom were not close to death. This makes this a landmark study, because it is the first to show that NDEs are associated with the patient actually being close to death or being temporarily clinically dead.

- The mean Greyson score for the NDE group (twenty-seven patients in total) was 12.7. Of the matched controls, twenty-one of the twenty-three achieved a score of 0, and two of the twenty-three scored 1. This finding extends to the wider non-experiencer population—96% of them scored 0 and 4% scored less than 5. This has clear implications. If there was a grey area in terms of the matched controls or non-experiencers having scores close to 7, the finding might suggest the NDE was possibly a physiological effect. However, there is no grey area here. There is a binary outcome with patients either scoring high numbers on the Greyson scale, or scoring nothing at all. Patients either had an NDE or they did not. There is no comparable experience induced by the similar medical situations.

- NDErs reported more prior paranormal experiences than the matched controls. Greyson notes, "Experiencers in this study did in fact report more prior purportedly paranormal experiences than did non-experiencers. That difference may suggest that persons who believe they had a paranormal experience are more likely to report NDEs; or it may suggest that persons who have NDEs are more likely to interpret past experiences as paranormal."

There is another explanation for this last observation. It is possible that subjects who have NDEs report more prior paranormal experiences because they are more "spiritual." There may be something about them, perhaps a genetic predisposition, that makes them more likely to have paranormal experiences and NDEs. Again, I offer a more in-depth discussion of the link between spirituality and genetics in Chapter 6.

STUDY 3: A QUALITATIVE AND QUANTITATIVE STUDY OF THE INCIDENCE, FEATURES AND ETIOLOGY OF NEAR-DEATH EXPERIENCES IN CARDIAC ARREST SURVIVORS.

Parnia, S. Resuscitation; 2001.

The author of this study is none other than Dr. Sam Parnia, whom I mentioned in this book's introduction. This study was, in many ways, the forerunner for the AWARE studies.

It was conducted at Southampton General Hospital in the UK over the course of one year at the end of the 1990s. It prospectively recruited cardiac arrest (CA) survivors, then interviewed the subjects within a week of the event and assessed any potential NDE memories using the Greyson scale. The investigators also recorded various physiological parameters, including hypoxia, electrolyte disturbances, and drugs, as well as psychological factors, such as religion, to determine whether there was an association between any of these parameters and reporting an NDE.

This study was one of a handful to prospectively deploy the use of "targets"—images on cards placed on high shelves in the resuscitation suite—to prove whether OBEs are indeed quantifiably genuine. According to Dr. Parnia: "If OBEs are indeed veridical, anybody who claimed to have left their body and be near the ceiling during a resuscitation attempt would be expected to identify those targets. If, however, such perceptions are psychological, then one would not expect the targets to be identified."

This statement is problematic for various reasons, one being that it is a rather crude summary of the experiment and not a fully developed hypothesis with respect to validation of the OBE. Moreover, it works on the assumption that staff won't see the cards and disclose to the patient what was on them. It also assumes that an NDEr was observing from the right place to notice the cards, or, even if they were in the same room. Having said that, this was a starting point in terms of experiments, and given this was in the 1990s, I don't think anyone at the time could have done better, and Dr Parnia is to be highly commended for undertaking a study of this kind in the first place. As it turns out, Parnia's comments about subjects observing targets was a moot point.

To briefly summarize, only four out of sixty-three CA subjects (6.3%) had an NDE according to the Greyson scale, which while not being 10%, was well within the bounds of error for such a small study. No significant differences in psychological or physiological factors were observed between those who experienced an NDE and those who did not. People who experienced an NDE had slightly higher levels of oxygen in the blood, but the numbers were too small to form a conclusive causative association. Given that four subjects reported an NDE, one might hope at least one subject would report an OBE given that about 25% of NDErs report OBEs. However, not only did no subjects report seeing the target cards, but there were no OBEs of any kind reported. This is why Parnia's statement is moot with respect to this study.

CHAPTER 3

THE AWARE STUDIES

It is now that the first destination on this journey appears on the horizon. We will soon be able to answer the question of whether there is enough evidence to validate OBEs and therefore NDEs.

At this point in the evolution of NDE science, an impasse has been reached. These three early prospective studies—and a multitude of other studies published in non-mainstream journals and books—were all saying the same things:

1. NDEs occur in about 10 percent of patients who experience a cardiac arrest.
2. NDErs report a number of core elements with a subset reporting visual and auditory OBEs.
3. A significant number of OBEs are veridical. Namely the observations made during the OBE were verified by another person, or persons,

who were often credible health care professionals with no personal relationship to the subject. One of these was reported within the setting of a clinical trial, and while this was not strictly speaking "scientifically verified" (proven using the scientific method), it does carry more weight than anecdotal accounts outside of a research setting.

In a normal world, despite the lack of scientifically measured proof, this should have been enough evidence to convince most reasonable people that NDEs and OBEs are real, and, in turn, all the implications that follow from that, including proving that humans have a consciousness that can survive death and "escape" the confines of the body. But, as I have noted, we live in a world ruled, for the most part, by materialist philosophy and its adherents. While these results were interesting to many who follow the field, numerous arguments have been presented by atheists within the academic establishment to explain away these results. None of these arguments address the impossibility of someone seeing or hearing things outside of their body, or even outside the room they were in, while they are unconscious. Instead they focus on whether the patients were truly unconscious or not, or whether the experiences were drug induced or hypoxia related hallucinations. Even if these arguments have validity, which as I will show later, they do not, they are a distraction from the central fact that even if the patients had their eyes open and were conscious, some of the veridical reports that were made would still be impossible by natural means. Worst of all, the competence, honesty, and integrity of the NDErs, the HCPs, and researchers who verified the OBEs is called into question. Skeptics want absolute proof that NDEs and OBEs are real and do not view human testimony from reliable sources as sufficient. Since then, those who are interested in this subject have been waiting for the AWARE studies to provide strong scientific evidence: evidence generated using the scientific method of hypothesis generation and experimentation.

AWARE I

Dr. Parnia did not launch the AWARE study until 2008, seven years after publishing the data from his initial study, possibly because he faced significant headwinds. Some in the medical scientific community opposed his work on NDEs, regarding it as frivolous or even quackery. He did not have big funding from the pharmaceutical industry, but he did receive support from the resuscitation council and from organizations such as the John Templeton and Nour foundations. More importantly he had to gain the support of numerous co-investigators from other hospitals to ensure there would be sufficiently speedy recruitment. As with all medical research involving patients, he was required to design the study in such a way that it passed the ethics review boards of the hospitals involved. Their role was to ensure the study would not place undue risk of any kind on patients. Given that patients who have just had a CA are probably not in the best of health and are in need of rest while they convalesce, having a researcher ask them questions about OBEs may have been regarded as an unnecessary intrusion and therefore potentially unethical. As a result, the questioning of subjects had to be designed in such a way that was sensitive to the health status of the patients.

The primary aim of the study was to establish the incidence of awareness and range of mental experiences during resuscitation and to establish a way of verifying reports of visual and auditory awareness during CA. In other words, to better understand how common NDEs are, what characterizes them, and how to prove whether or not they are real.

The study was a multi-center, international, prospective observational study. It took place in twenty hospitals around the world, but mostly in the UK and US. It recruited patients who had a CA and, if possible, were able to give an interview, provided they were deemed sufficiently fit by their care provider and had consented to taking part in the study. The aim was to interview the CA survivors in person before leaving hospital if possible, but if not, by telephone shortly afterward.

To validate the visual component of NDEs, each hospital installed 50–100 shelves in locations where CPR was likely to occur, such as ER wards. Each shelf had different images including such things as animals, religious symbols, people, and newspaper headlines that were only visible from above if viewed from the ceiling. In the early pilot stages of the study, which took place in five hospitals, HCPs involved in resuscitating the patient were asked to mention out loud three cities or three colors during the procedure, in order to validate auditory recollections. In reality, this proved very hard to remember to do and was abandoned once the study enrolled more centers.

Where possible, consenting patients underwent a potential sequence of three interviews. In the first interview, demographic questions addressing age, race, education, etc., were asked. In addition, it was established whether or not they had any recollections of consciousness during their CA. If they had any of the latter, then they had a second interview in which they underwent a Greyson scale evaluation. As with many other studies, the recollections were classified as an NDE if they had a score of 7 or more. Finally, if patients reported memories of seeing or hearing things during their CA, they undertook a third interview to ascertain any details they could recall.

The initial goal was to recruit 1,000 to 1,500 patients. This was deemed to be a sufficient number of survivors to generate enough recollections of awareness that would better characterize the experiences. To me, based on assumptions I made about who was included in the study, this seemed like a reasonable number considering that data from previous studies showed about 10% of CA survivors have an NDE, and of these, about 20–25% have a visual OBE. Based on that, if one thousand patients were recruited, I would have expected to see about one hundred NDEs and twenty-five OBEs, and you would expect that if that many people reported OBEs, and if OBEs were indeed real, a few of those would catch sight of and recall a target image on a shelf (maybe 10–20%).

However, it is important to note that while it was the desire of people like myself for this study to validate NDEs through scientifically proving that OBEs occur, this was not explicitly stated as being the aim of the AWARE study. Therefore, the paper did not contain a clearly defined hypothesis providing a potential explanation for OBEs. This in turn meant that the objectives and design of the study relating to this aspect were a bit woolly. In a situation with no constraints from the skeptical medical community, the study would ideally have been designed around the following specific hypothesis:

Hypothesis 1: OBEs are a result of the consciousness persisting after the heart has stopped beating and brain activity has ceased. It therefore follows that the consciousness is a separate entity from the body, independent of brain function, and is able to survive death for an indeterminate period.

If this hypothesis had been explicitly stated by Dr. Parnia, then the experiment/study would have been designed in such a way as to focus on attempting to produce a sufficient number of OBEs to determine if they were real, along the lines of the numbers I mentioned above. However, as I will show you, the study was not designed with such a clear hypothesis or objectives. In reality, the study was, as described in its aims: an observational study with the goals of determining frequency of awareness and *identifying* methods for validating auditory and visual recollections, rather than explicitly setting out to *use* these methods to validate OBEs. It was not a study with the specific aim of validating the veracity of OBEs. This is a fundamental point when it comes to discussing the results.

Finally, before discussing the results, I would generate an additional and very important hypothesis or statement related to this research, but one that would never be included in a medical study. The important implications of this will be discussed in detail after we have reviewed the results from the AWARE studies.

Hypothesis 2: If OBEs are proven to be real, then, by inference, so too are the other core elements of NDEs.

AWARE I: RESULTS

Dr. Parnia presented the AWARE I study results on a poster at a cardiology conference in 2014, and shortly after, published them in the journal called Resuscitation.[16]

The study "recruited" 2,060 patients, which was considerably more than the initial 1000–1500 patients originally planned. I put *recruited* in quotes because this a somewhat misleading description. Based on data from previous studies, as well as assumptions I made about the inclusion and exclusion criteria of the study (the predefined criteria that would determine if a subject could be enrolled or not), I would have expected that out of 2,060 subjects, two hundred would have NDEs and about fifty patients would have OBEs. If the primary hypothesis outlined above is true, maybe six to ten CA survivors would have verified OBEs by observing and identifying the images on the cards.

The actual result? There was only one verified OBE, and it was not verified using the cards.

The results of the study were obviously disappointing from the perspective of those hoping for "smoking gun" evidence. At first glance, it failed to fully

---

16   Parnia S, et al. AWARE—AWAreness during REsuscitation—A prospective study. Resuscitation (2014).

validate the hypothesis I describe above and thereby support the belief that OBEs weren't real, and the consciousness did not leave the body at death.

So what went wrong?

After an in-depth review, it became obvious that AWARE I had been extremely unlikely to verify OBEs with Dr. Parnia's card system, and there were a number of reasons why. Ultimately, it was to do with fundamental aspects of the design and powering of the study that arise from not creating the experiment with the primary intent of scientifically verifying OBEs, like the one I propose. If you don't specifically set out to look for something, then you are much less likely to find it.

Firstly, were there really enough subjects in the study to sufficiently power it?

If 2,060 CA survivors had been interviewed, and their CAs and CPR had occurred in rooms with image shelves, then as stated above, you'd expect maybe five to ten fully verified OBEs. But there were none, so either the hypothesis is wrong, or there weren't, in fact, a sufficient number of patients. I wouldn't be writing this book if it was the former.

The vast majority of the 2,060 patients did not survive long enough to be interviewed by the study investigators. Only 140 patients reached the first of the interview stages. That's right, only 140 CA survivors were actually interviewed. If the study had been designed around the specific hypothesis I propose, then the minimum requirements for being included in the analysis would be that they survived long enough to complete the interviews. The objective would have been to recruit one thousand patients who reached this stage. However, only a fraction made it that far.

How many NDEs might we expect to be reported from a group of 140 patients who had been revived after having a CA? About fourteen, given that 10% percent in previous studies had NDEs. In fact, nine people in total had recollections that exceeded 7 on the Greyson scale and were classified as NDEs Given that about 25% of NDErs report OBEs, we would expect two to three of these nine to report OBEs. Two people reported seeing or hearing things during their NDE. Given that one of the study's objectives was to determine the incidence of NDEs during CA, they got some of the way toward achieving this, although arguably they only confirmed what had been noted in previous studies. And while nine out of 140 is only 6% of people reporting an NDE versus 10% from previous studies, it is well within the bounds of error given the small number of actual participants. If they had actually recruited one thousand CA survivors and still arrived at an incidence of 6%, then this number would be regarded as more reliable than the numbers generated from the previous, smaller studies. But with 140 subjects, it is too small a sample to make definitive conclusions. The number of OBEs is very much in line with what has been observed before, but it is also irrelevant in informing the field due to the tiny sample size. However, that doesn't necessarily answer the question of why weren't either of the OBEs verified by the patients seeing the cards.

Firstly, using target cards is a relatively limited and crude way of verifying OBEs, as not all patients who have an OBE report seeing themselves from directly above. Sometimes they are standing beside themselves or are in the corner of the room. It is hard to estimate what the chances are of someone experiencing an OBE and having it from the right vantage point to see the cards.

Secondly, due to the fact that OBEs are an unusual and unexpected event, it is possible, maybe even likely, that the experiencer may not have the "presence of mind" to notice the cards, even if they were in a position where they were able to see them. Given this, I estimate perhaps only 10–20% of people who have OBEs might see and remember the cards. This is something that would need to be considered in the design of the experiment, as well as why you would need in excess of one thousand CA survivors reaching the interview stage. Given that only two people reported OBEs, it is unlikely that one or both of two patients who had OBEs would have seen and remembered the cards …if they had even been in rooms with cards in the first place.

Thirdly, and of most relevance to answering the question of why didn't any patients identify the cards, is the fact that despite there being over one thousand "card shelves" in multiple hospital sites in acute and emergency wards, 78% of the CAs that occurred during this study occurred in patients' rooms without the shelves. As a result, neither of the patients who reported OBEs were in rooms with cards present.

The only verified OBE in the AWARE I study was that of a man who made observations from the corner of a room while his body was unconscious on a bed. In his interview he was able to identify staff who were only present in the room while he was unconscious, as well as being able to describe in detail many of the procedures that were performed. His accounts were verified by members of the team who performed the emergency resuscitation process. This is a very good example of a well-documented, humanly verified, veridical OBE, but with the exception that it was recorded in the setting of a prospective clinical study looking out for this effect, and that the events he reported were correlated with the time that he was reported to be clinically dead.

Given the context of the setting of the recorded OBE, there are arguments for and against naming this a "scientifically" validated OBE. What is the argument for? The study was created using the scientific method, conducted in a scientific manner in a research setting and an OBE was confirmed by reliable professional human observers and for the first time the observations made by the subject were matched with the time he would not have been able to make or record observations since he was clinically dead.

The argument against is that it failed to verify OBEs using the pre-specified technique designed for the purpose of validating visual observations during

CPR. As a scientist, I am of the view that the latter position is correct. While one of the OBEs was verified in an extremely credible manner, it was not "scientifically" verified. It is important to note that the OBE was not scientifically disproved either, the study just failed to collect enough information to allow a conclusion to be drawn on this subject. To get sufficient data to inform us on the scientific validity of OBEs would have required making this objective a primary endpoint. If they had done that, they would have made it a goal to have at least five hundred to one thousand post CA interviews.

While it might seem that I am being somewhat critical of the study investigators, in particular Sam Parnia, I want to stress that I am absolutely not criticizing them - in fact I hold Sam Parnia and his fellow researchers in nothing but the highest regard for their immense contribution to the field. Any missteps can attributed to the fact they were building the airplane while learning to fly.

I am just explaining why the study failed to produce scientific verification of whether or not OBEs are genuine experiences in which the consciousness observes events from outside of the body. In reality, Dr. Parnia did not have the resources or the time to conduct a study that would have needed to be at least five times larger than it was. The largest hurdle facing Dr. Parnia was in fact the lack of people surviving CAs.

Having learned about his techniques from AWARE I, Sam Parnia went on to perform the follow-up study, AWARE II. Let's take a closer look ...

*

AWARE II

Over the year following the AWARE I study, details emerged about the design of the next study: AWARE II. It was hoped that the suggestions that were made after critiquing the design of AWARE I would have been included in the design of this new study, but unfortunately, some of the more important ones weren't. Regardless, the primary goal of the clinical study would be to collect different measures of what happens to the brain during resuscitation and thereby assess the health and activity of the brain during and after CPR. This is largely dependent on how much oxygenated blood is reaching the brain. The secondary goal of the study was to ascertain the presence of consciousness during CA and the occurrence of OBEs and NDEs. By measuring the oxygen levels using oximetry and the electrical activity using EEG, it would be possible to correlate any conscious recollections with concurrent physiological parameters.

The study sought to recruit 1,000–1,500 patients and had slightly tightened the inclusion criteria—the specific characteristics of the subjects that could be enrolled. Subjects needed to have an in-hospital CA when the AWARE research team were present and the AWARE study equipment was in place during CPR and before ROSC. The team also made several important alterations to the methodology used to verify any potential OBE reports. They abandoned the shelves with cards for a much more modern and scientifically robust technique, including the addition of auditory measurements.

Any auditory confirmation of consciousness is every bit as valid as visual confirmation. When one hears, auditory nerves in the cochlea convert sound waves into an electrical signal that is sent to the brain. The brain then "translates" this electrical signal into something our consciousness understands as a sound. The same is true for nerves in the eye for sight, or nose for smell, or skin for touch. When a sensory nerve is exposed to an external stimulus, it sends an electrical signal to the brain, which then interprets that signal into something the consciousness "experiences." Given this understanding, it is easy to perceive consciousness as separate from the physical world yet connected to it by the body when it receives physical stimuli relayed to the brain. The brain could be seen as the physical "interface" between the body and consciousness. It interprets the external data passed to it along the various nerves connected to sensors around the body, so our consciousness is able to experience the external environment.

In other words, the human consciousness hears with its brain, not its ears. That may sound odd, but it is fundamentally true. While the sound is received by the ears, we only hear it if our brain processes the signal from the auditory nerve, and we will only remember the sound if our consciousness is active and able to process the sound into a memory. Both of these are higher functions of the brain and require significant activity, therefore if the EEG is flat and there are no physical signs of consciousness, reports of hearing sounds during this period are evidence of the consciousness persisting beyond death and being independent of the body and the brain.

Special crash carts or trolleys that carry equipment commonly used for emergency resuscitation were designed to monitor patients during the AWARE II study. These carts carried equipment investigators would use to specifically analyze activity in the patient's brain post-CA and during resuscitation. Then they'd correlate the information with any reports of conscious activity, and alongside ascertaining clinical implications, potentially verify, or discount, any reported OBEs. This included oximetry machines which measure oxygen levels and thereby blood flow to the brain and EEG monitors, which show actual brain activity. They are the key physiological parameters that determine the effectiveness of CPR and the brain's capacity to generate, or host, consciousness. For example, if the EEG is below a certain level, conscious processes cannot occur[17]. There was also equipment to produce visual and auditory stimuli during resuscitation to assess the patient's external awareness during any conscious episodes. This included headphones to place on the patient's ears to convey loud sounds and an iPad fixed to a pole above head height with the screen facing the ceiling, which would produce random images only visible from above the iPad's screen.

In previous NDE reports some patients claimed to hear things while clinically dead. The computer producing loud sounds in the headphones would cross reference any patient reports of hearing these sounds with the timed record of physiological outputs, such as EEG activity. By doing this, the reports could be matched to the timed data from the EEG, thus making it possible to draw very specific conclusions about the effectiveness of CPR, and the presence of consciousness. Beyond any clinical implications, if the patient heard a specific noise at a moment when the EEG proved their brain was physically incapable of hearing things, this would validate any reports of consciousness independent of the brain or body and be regarded as a confirmed auditory OBE. This would represent genuine scientific validation of the OBE phenomenon because the experiment designed to test the OBE hypothesis generated a measurable, technologically verified result.

With regard to the confirmation of visual OBEs, things are much more straightforward. The only way patients could see what was on the iPad is if they had an OBE. The issue is whether or not they *would* see it. If patients left their body and were directly above themselves, as many have claimed, the images

---

17   The measure of conscious activity is broken down into different brain waves. Alpha waves (8 to 12 Hz) are dominant during quiet thoughts and in some meditative states; beta waves (13 to 32 Hz) dominate our normal waking state of consciousness when attention is directed towards cognitive tasks and the outside world; and gamma waves (33 to 100 Hz) are the fastest brain waves, and relate to simultaneous processing of information from different brain areas. Delta waves (0.1 to 3.5 Hz) are associated with deep sleep and not conscious awareness.

displayed on the ipad screen should be difficult to miss. In my estimation, 30 to 50% of patients experiencing a visual OBE would see the image if the crash cart and iPad screen was positioned in such a way that it was visible and obvious from directly above the body, as is the case in AWARE II.

Importantly, when it comes to inclusion criteria, the patients would only be included in the study if the crash cart had arrived before the patient was resuscitated. This was an attempt to avoid the situation that happened in AWARE I, where OBEs occurred without the images being present. Of equal importance is the fact that because this study is primarily designed for assessing the health of the brain during and after CPR, it does not exclude patients who die before an interview can be conducted. Data collected on oxygen levels and EEG activity during CPR will be informative from a medical perspective, irrespective of whether the patient survives or not. This is the kind of research that Dr Parnia and his lab performs that result in advances in CPR techniques and are important for improving emergency room treatments and saving lives.

Once again, it appears there is no specific hypothesis relating to OBEs in this iteration of AWARE, but my original hypothesis still stands: if OBEs are proved real, then consciousness separates from the body at death and survives beyond death.

2022 CONSENSUS STATEMENT[18]

Before we look at the results from AWARE II, it is important to address another publication that Parnia and other eminent NDE researchers published in early 2022. This was a consensus statement that attempted to summarize the state of the field and to clearly define the characteristics of what differentiates "authentic" NDEs and OBEs from other experiences. The authors, led by Sam Parnia, stated that due to the evolution of the field from its early days in the 1970s, the term NDE has become too broad and now includes experiences that are not strictly associated with death, to the extent that people have been mislabeling experiences such as hallucinations due to psychedelic drug, or CPR induced consciousness (CPRIC), as NDEs.

The first proposal coming out of the consensus was to rename the two best known acronyms – NDE and OBE, to RED (recalled experience of death) and EVA (external visual awareness).

REDs, also now known as authentic NDEs, could only be called REDs if they included the following components:

- A relation with death,
- a sense of transcendence,
- ineffability (cannot be described in words),
- positive transformative effects (related to meaning and purpose to life), and a
- severity of illness that leads to loss of consciousness (LOC), together with
- the absence of features of other coma-related experiences (such as conventional dreams, delirium, and delusions, in the intensive care unit (ICU) or elsewhere)

---

18 Guidelines and standards for the study of death and recalled experiences of death--a multidisciplinary consensus statement and proposed future directions; Parnia, S. Et al; N.Y. Acad. Sci. xxxx (2022) 1–17)

They suggested that the first 4 components relate to the "narrative arc" that has been described in the various core indices. This narrative arc comprises the following sequence of experiences:

- Separation (from the body)
- Heading to a "destination"
- Reliving the recording of my life: actions and intentions matter
- "Home" again – as in the place the consciousness ends up feels like home…not here
- The return
- Reported effects after the experience

Each of these in turn has a number of key characteristics, which expand on the core experiences of the Greyson scale.

The reason I have included this here is that the data from the 2023 AWARE II publication uses this terminology and these criteria. While I understand why Parnia et al have created the new acronym, I am not convinced it is the right one to use because of the standard definition of the word death as being irreversible, as opposed to the clinical definition where it is regarded as a treatable condition. This semantic inaccuracy opens up these accounts to the reasonable accusation that the experiencers "weren't really dead". If they had used RECD, recalled experiences of clinical death, then this would be precise but less catchy. In my view Near Death better describes the condition, therefore for the rest of this book I will continue using NDE. Moreover, the term NDE is one which people are familiar with and I have defined what an NDE is when I refer to it. There are two other aspects of the consensus paper that I disagree with, and one of those, the idea that an experience can only be a RED if it is positive, actually goes against the literature that Parnia cites to use this definition. The other relates to memory. Both of these issues will be covered in sections later, but suffice to say it appears that Parnia only wants to believe in a universe where everyone gets a happy ending. By narrowing the future of research in this field to only positive experiences when there are quite clearly Hell-like experiences that share many of the other key characteristics of NDEs, he is creating a very dangerous precedent and potentially denying mankind of some extremely important and pertinent information about the future of the soul. As I have said before, I have a lot of respect for him and the team who work with him, but on this issue and on the issue of memory, I disagree. That is why this book is so important because no one else is discussing what is a potentially catastrophic outcome for a significant percentage of people who will inevitably die.

I will return to this later, but now for a discussion of the results from AWARE II.

AWARE II PUBLICATION SUMMER 2023[19]

This section contains material that was taken directly from or adapted from the publication, along with my commentary:

METHODS:

These are mostly along the lines of what was detailed earlier in this section, but with some aspects that were clarified in the publication:

Given the 5-10% probability of CA survival with many survivors unable to undergo interviews, the AWARE II study combined a prospective and cross-sectional design. The prospective arm was used to:

---

19   AWAreness during REsuscitation - II: A multi-center study of consciousness and awareness in cardiac arrest; Parnia et al. Resuscitation, July 7, 2023

i. identify the incidence and categories of recalled cognitive themes,
ii. establish sub-studies of implicit learning and explicit recall, and
iii. pilot-test brain monitoring systems.

This prospective part actively recruited patients who were having CA after the study started and collected data on them. The cross-sectional arm aimed to overcome the limitation of low survival in the prospective arm, by providing a larger population of survivors with memories for qualitative analysis of the themes and breadth of CA-related experiences. This part of the study looked at NDE reports that were self-reported outside the context of a scientific study and I will not say much about it as I feel it was a last minute add-on for reasons which will become apparent and that have plagued previous studies.

The rest of this discussion relates to the prospective part of the study which is the one that is most relevant.

Patients were recruited consecutively during working hours. Inclusion criteria:

1. age≥18 years,
2. IHCA (In Hospital Cardiac Arrest) lasting≥5 minutes.

EXCLUSION: OUT-OF-HOSPITAL CARDIAC ARREST (OHCA).

At first glance the IHCA lasting more than 5 minutes seems a bit arbitrary and given that we don't know how long someone needs to be in CA before their NDE/OBE begins, places a severe constraint on the study. This is exacerbated by the fact that many people who survive IHCA will be resuscitated quickly, sometimes within a few minutes of CA, and that the longer they go without ROSC, the lower the chances of survival. Moreover, many who have extended OBEs may have had a brief period in CA, but once ROSC has been achieved stay physically unconscious, but still continue to have experiences.

The primary outcome was visual or auditory consciousness/awareness during CA.

Secondary outcomes were:

1. EEG biomarkers of consciousness,
2. implicit learning using audiovisual tests of awareness

Survivors potentially underwent a three-stage interview process:

- Stage-1 interviews regarding their perceptions of awareness and memories during CPR
- Stage-2 interviews probed the nature of experiences using NDE scale
- Stage-3 interviews were for patients with auditory and visual recollections.

Depending on recovery, survivors were interviewed ~2-4 weeks after CA. Regarding the previously mentioned crash cart, a tablet-computer was taken to IHCA and clamped above the patient's head, with the screen above the field of view of staff and away from chest compressions. The headphones were placed over the ears during CPR. One minute after being switched on, the tablet randomly projected one of 10 stored images onto its screen, and after five minutes 6-10 audio cues (three fruits: apple-pear- banana) were delivered to the headphones every minute for five minutes. For analysis of explicit recall, survivors were asked to recall memories, including audiovisual stimuli during CPR. To test for implicit learning, survivors were asked to randomly select one image (from 10) and also randomly state the names of any three fruits they thought were present during CPR.

RESULTS:

Of 567 subjects, 213(37.6%) achieved sustained ROSC, 53(9.3%) survived to discharge. Due to poor health, only 28/53 completed interviews. During stage 1-2 interviews, 11/28(39%), reported memories and/or perceptions from CA. Using the near-death scale, 6/28(21%) had a transcendent experience. There were no reports of external signs of consciousness (groaning, moving, rolling).

Importantly no one had explicit recall of the projected images or auditory cues. One subject was able to remember the fruits through implicit recall (i.e. they could not remember hearing the words, but associated the fruits with time during CA).

Let's stop there and determine what all this means.

Firstly, this study suffered from the same fundamental issue as previous studies, namely low numbers of interviews due to the low survival rates of people experiencing CA. There was an additional confounding factor in this study…COVID. The study effectively stopped recruiting in March 2020 when all the research staff were pulled off this study and into COVID work. As a result, rather than recruiting 1500 patients as originally intended, they only recruited 567, and when I say recruited, once again this term is meaningless since the vast majority sadly did not survive to discharge and were therefore unable to be interviewed. In fact, only 28 qualified to be included in the study and survived to interview. Of these 6 had NDEs, but none reported an OBE. The truth is that this is a worse outcome than AWARE I, but it does not in any way imply that OBEs or NDEs are not real.

Not only were there a lower number of interviews than AWARE I, but the likelihood is that they may have missed a number of potential NDEs/OBEs due to the inclusion criteria. I am not sure why they needed to be in CA for at least 5 minutes, but as mentioned above, this may have proved a constraining factor. Possibly related to this was the fact that it usually took about 4 minutes for the adapted crash cart to arrive to the IHCA and then another minute or two for everything to be hooked up and started. The study is still ongoing, but it may be another 5 years before we get any more results and an OBE.

The other aspect of the results that was intriguing was the EEG sub study, and the conclusions that Sam Parnia drew from this data.

EEG data "consistent with consciousness" was recorded in patients up to 60 minutes after CA began, although in truth the majority of this EEG activity was not in fact consistent with lucid consciousness. The most important aspect of the EEG findings relates to whether any of the patients who reported NDEs also had EEG output consistent with consciousness. If there was a single patient who had EEG data consistent with consciousness while having an NDE, then at the very least it would be possible to claim there is a relationship between these experiences and brain activity. That could have two possible explanations:

1. The brain is possibly causing the NDE thus supporting the hypothesis that the soul is not an independent entity, or
2. As the consciousness is leaving the brain it causes an increase in brain activity. Parnia refers to this as disinhibition (I call it "the soul packing its bags and leaving" hypothesis).

However, neither of these is relevant in this instance since the paper states:

"Two of 28 interviewed subjects had EEG data but weren't among those with explicit cognitive recall."

This is the money line. This is the one that shoots down any materialist attempts to use this study to say that NDEs are proven to be a result of brain activity (and there will be lots of attempts).

Not one of the 11 subjects who reported conscious recollections, including the 6 who had NDEs, had any EEG data, let alone EEG data that showed markers of consciousness. Because of this it is entirely false to use this paper (or other studies that show EEG activity after CA without an associated NDE report) to claim there is an association of brain activity with NDEs or with consciousness during CPR. If anything, the fact that the only 2 patients out of the 28 interviewed who had EEG data had no recall points to the EEG data not being related to conscious activity, or at the least the ability to remember conscious activity.

Given this, it is all the more baffling that the study authors make the following arguments in the discussion:

"Recent reports of a surge of gamma and other physiological electrical activity (ordinarily seen with lucid consciousness) during and after cardiac standstill and death, led to speculation that biomarker(s) of lucidity at death may exist, which our findings support. Taken together, these studies and ours provide a novel understanding of how lucid experiences in relation to cardiac standstill/death may arise. Ischemic depolarization may initiate brain disinhibition - leading to activation of dormant pathways - observed as transient electrocortical biomarkers of lucidity. Although of unknown evolutionary benefit, instead of being hallucinatory, illusory or delusional, this appears to facilitate lucid understanding of new dimensions of reality – including people's deeper consciousness - all memories, thoughts, intentions and actions towards others from a moral and ethical perspective. The mechanism of consciousness and its relationship with brain resuscitation and function remain undiscovered. "Bottom-up" or "top-down" mechanisms are proposed for the emergence of consciousness. The former considers consciousness as an epiphenomenon from brain activities; the latter, as a separate undiscovered entity not produced by understood brain mechanisms, which can independently modulate brain activity. The

identification of potential electrocortical biomarkers of consciousness doesn't resolve this conundrum, as an association doesn't imply causation. However, the paradoxical finding of lucidity and heightened reality when brain function is severely disordered, or has ceased raises the need to consider alternatives to the epiphenomenon theory."

In simple terms they are suggesting that the EEG data from AWARE II, when combined with EEG data from a study in rats and another in coma patients, points to a possible mechanism by which these experiences occur. Specifically, Dr Parnia is saying, and has said more explicitly and definitively in interviews at the back end of 2023, that these EEG signals are the result of the brain disinhibiting and accessing new dimensions of reality. In this paper he used the word "may" but in the various interviews with the likes of the BBC, CNN and the Guardian he states it as though it is factually proven.

Fine, speculate, but there is no evidential basis for this assertion. There is not a single case of EEG activity during CA associated with either an NDE or conscious recollection of any kind. It is groundless speculation, a hypothesis without evidence. There are however two cases of EEG data with no conscious recollections, but this is being ignored.

It isn't even like he is committing the sin of using association to imply causation, he is going a step further because there is not even any association! The worst thing is that none of the interviewers picked up on this or dug deeper and the more Dr Parnia says the brain activity is the brain disinhibiting and accessing other dimensions the more it seems to be accepted. However, as I was writing this section it appears I was not alone in observing this since two of the great researchers in this area, Pim Van Lommel and Bruce Greyson also commented that he had overstepped the mark causing him to publish a response in the journal where he published AWARE II[20].

The fact that patients undergoing CPR who were in CA had EEG activity

---

20   https://doi.org/10.1016/j.resuscitation.2023.110080

is of itself a groundbreaking discovery as this has not been observed to this extent before, but to say it means anything specific about the presence of consciousness feels misleading (unless he has further data). There are a few possible explanations for the emergence of brain activity during CA:

1. Parnia's disinhibition theory (this then possibly leads to dissociation of the consciousness from the brain and the subsequent aspects of an NDE)
2. The brain is producing conscious activity,
3. The brain is starting up sporadically due to blood flow from CPR.

Personally, while I like the idea of the disinhibition hypothesis, and that at some point the consciousness must separate from the brain possibly causing EEG activity, I am of the view that the activity observed in this study is more likely related to number 3. All of these patients were undergoing CPR, and it is likely that at certain points sufficient oxygenated blood reached the brain to cause it to start rebooting. I don't know that, but I would argue given what I said above, this is the most likely explanation of the EEG activity.

SUMMARY:

While the data presented in the paper published in September 2023 on the AWARE II study is truly groundbreaking, in that it showed that there can be brain activity consistent with conscious activity while in CA and undergoing CPR, there was no scientifically verified OBE. This is not very surprising given the small number of interviews and the fact that the crash cart took five minutes after CA to arrive and begin the experiments.

The fact is that most NDEs follow a chronological sequence. CA > OBE with patient observing body > tunnel > dead relatives/heavenly realms/Being of light. Parnia calls this a narrative arc. While the NDEr is in the first OBE state, they are in this dimension of time, and from the descriptions I have read they tend not to hang around very long, although a few do. This possibly means the cart was unlikely to be in the room when a subject was having an OBE.

As for the EEG data pointing towards some sort of disinhibition mechanism…I have said enough.

While disappointing, there is hope that we may not have to wait so long for a scientifically verified OBE:

AWARE III

This is a study in patients who undergo hypothermic surgery, also conducted by the AWARE group, which is perhaps one of the more promising in terms of getting verified OBEs. In this kind of surgery, critical work is done on the heart or the brain where the surgeon must cool the body temperature down to the point that the patient experiences deep hypothermic circulatory arrest. This causes the patient's heart to stop beating and the brain to stop functioning. This state can be maintained for about an hour without any ill effects because the cells in the brain are cooled sufficiently to avoid any damage. Once the hour is up, the patient is then warmed up and revived. It is a well-established, relatively safe and reliable technique.

Interestingly, and perhaps unsurprisingly given that the patients are, in essence, clinically dead, there have been a number of reports of OBEs during these medical procedures. Pam Reynolds' NDE, mentioned earlier, and in the next section, is one example. Another was noted in a study in Montreal specifically set up to investigate this phenomenon[21].

This study also found that about 10% of people had conscious recollections that mirrored results from "natural" cardiac arrest NDEs.

---

21   VOLUME 83, ISSUE 1, E19 2012. Conscious mental activity during a deep hypothermic cardiocirculatory arrest? Mario Beauregard

As AWARE III gets under way, Dr. Parnia is going to use his setup with the iPad and headphones in hypothermic surgeries. Given that the patients will almost certainly survive and may have consented to the study prior to "dying," they may even be asked to look for the iPad, if they have an OBE. It is possible however, that the study may not yield any results due to changes in technique since the Montreal study. A similar recent study had no NDEs or OBEs. We will see, Parnia's new study recruited its first patient in July 2020.

There is a more fundamental question though, and one that I have been asking more and more of late:

DO WE REALLY NEED A "SCIENTIFICALLY" VERIFIED OBE?

This is a question I have touched on before and will refer back to again at times. As a physical scientist who works in medicine, until recently, I have only been one hundred percent confident of the results of an experiment when it is confirmed by technological measurements. For instance, during my years working in HIV, we would use measurements of viral load (amount of virus in a ml of blood), and CD4 count (numbers of the CD4 immune cells in a ml of blood) to measure the effectiveness of a drug. When I worked in Alzheimer's there were two ways of testing the effectiveness of a drug. One was using MRI and PET scans to see the change in brain structure and presence of two types of protein - Amyloid and Tau; the other was a cognitive test usually carried out by psychiatrist. Both of these are highly objective, quantitative and scientific, even the cognitive test which uses a battery of specific questions that track changes in the patient's ability to remember things and to process information. The answers to these questions are objectively measurable. For example, in the Mini Mental State Exam (MMSE) you are asked to remember three words at the end of the meeting that were read out loud at the start. There is no subjective interpretation from the psychiatrist...the score for this segment of the test is 0-3.

The results from any of these tests I have described are not questioned as they have been validated in studies and, especially with scans and blood tests, avoid any human potential interference through subjective interpretation, or manipulation. Of course, statisticians can fiddle with numbers and create different impressions, but such antics are easily exposed by the eagle eyed.

All of the therapy areas I have worked in up to this point in my career have had scientific objective measures to validate results, however more recently I have been in discussions with an organisation that has developed a drug that treats depression. In this instance, as with Alzheimer's, a psychiatrist will have a battery of questions to ask a patient, but unlike with the cognitive tests used in Alzheimer's which have clear objectively measurable responses to each question, the answers are much more down to subjective interpretation by the patient or psychiatrist. For instance, when using the Montgomery-Asberg Depression Rating Scale (MADRS), a patient may be asked to describe their state of inner tension, which can cover any number of symptoms including feelings of ill-defined discomfort, edginess, inner turmoil, mental tension mounting to either panic, dread, etc. These qualitative measures are completely unlike any tests I have relied on before to prove or disprove a hypothesis about a drug. They are subjective descriptors which entirely rely on human testimony and observation, AND YET, leading doctors, scientists, health bodies, insurance companies, government regulators etc will accept the results from these questionnaires as having objective definitive meaning regarding the effectiveness of drugs that target depression. In other words, the medical, scientific and academic establishment accept these results as being reliable, even "scientifically" verified, despite them being entirely based on subjective human testimony.

Maybe you can see where I am going with this!

There are countless OBEs that have been recalled by patients after suffering

CA, and have been corroborated by healthcare professionals, many of whom were licensed physicians. What is so different from the results of a clinical trial in depression, or indeed a psychiatrist conducting an MADRS test on a patient for the purpose of an insurance claim for medication or a period of absence? You have:

- a subject accurately describing things they saw while "out of their bodies" that they could not possibly have seen with their physical bodies. They rarely go straight to the local TV station and recount their story, or even write about it. They will usually tell hospital staff first.

- These recollections are then verified as accurate, and only possible if the patient had indeed been out of their body, by reliable rational scientifically minded professionals involved in the case. These professionals have nothing to gain by confirming these recollections, and indeed may be the subject of derision from colleagues.

Just as with measuring depression, you have a subjective patient account and an HCP evaluating that account. We have thousands of these.

Here are 7 well known cases that are condensed from the full accounts to capture the key criteria that cause them to be fully validated OBEs. These two criteria are:

1. An observation by a patient of a specific object, procedure, event that they claimed to see while they were having their OBE and which happened during CA or in a coma following CA.

2. The account was confirmed by an identifiable HCP and, ideally, the HCP stated that this was only possible if the patient had indeed had an OBE as their eyes were closed and their vitals pointed to an absence of physical consciousness.

While these seven cases are well known, there are countless others. Over one hundred are presented in the book: *The Self does not die*. I have used this book as the main reference source due to the fact that all the cases are well documented and were investigated by the authors who interviewed all the witnesses, including HCPs, that were involved in the confirmed OBEs. However, I have been familiar with many of these cases over the years and most are presented elsewhere, including on YouTube. Even these hundred odd are just the tip of the iceberg, but just happened to have HCPs who were prepared to go on the record and had sufficiently robust corroborating evidence. I recommend buying the book as a reference source if you are interested in this area. A couple of these cases have been mentioned before:

PAM REYNOLDS (SINGER/SONGWRITER 1956-2010):

Circumstances: Occurred in 1991 at the Barrow Neurological Institute during brain surgery while Reynolds was in a state of hypothermic cardiac arrest. The operating physician was neurosurgeon Dr Robert Spetzler. The 2 criteria:

1. Reynolds had an OBE in which she saw a part of the operation on her brain, and specifically saw highly specialised equipment (a saw that looked like a toothbrush) being used, as well as other details that would have required observing the procedure from outside of her body. Moreover, she heard detailed discussions about the procedure that would have been impossible to hear naturally due to headphones being in her ears that played loud sounds and were designed to completely exclude external noise.

2. The account was confirmed by Robert Spetzler, a pioneer of the hypothermic CA method, and an internationally respected neurosurgeon. He discounted the possibility that she might have

guessed these things from watching TV shows, or reading up on the surgical techniques and he could not provide a "normal explanation" for what had occurred.

DR LLOYD RUDY'S CASE:

I first came across this on YouTube. Its authenticity struck me because it was buried in a channel for people interested in dental surgery, and was a spontaneous account of an OBE given to the channel's host by the highly respected, and well known Cardiac Surgeon, Dr Lloyd Rudy, in 2011 during which they also discussed cardiac problems related to dental infections. All the other videos, which averaged about 300 views, were of the same format with the same host. This wasn't a channel devoted to NDEs, of which there are many. Despite its esoteric location, the video had millions of views by the time I first came across it. In this instance we don't know the identity of the patient, and it was Lloyd Rudy who reported the account, not long before his own death in 2012.

Circumstances: Occurred on a Christmas Day in an unspecified year in a hospital in Great Falls. An oral infection had spread to a heart valve of the patient, resulting in Dr Rudy performing cardiac surgery. The surgery seemed to fail and the life support machines were turned off and the various staff had begun leaving the theatre. Suddenly, after the patient's chest had been sown up ready for autopsy, some of the patient's vitals started to return, and once all the staff had rushed back to the theatre the patient's blood pressure and heart rate were normalised. He had effectively come back from the dead with no CPR. It is very rare, but does happen, and may account for some of the rare historic NDEs prior to the invention of CPR. The patient had been completely unconscious during the surgery and was in a coma for 2 days after the restoration of vital functions. The 2 criteria:

1. The patient reported a number of incidents during the surgery that he could not have seen, including seeing a series of post it notes on a monitor. These notes were put on the monitor for Dr Rudy by a nurse who had taken messages he needed to respond to after the surgery. They were placed there after the surgery began and removed straight after it was finished.

2. Given this account was actually provided by Dr Rudy, this criterion is already fulfilled. He stated there was no way he could have naturally seen this as the patient "was out" before the operation began.

This discussion between Dr Rudy and the interviewer, who is a dental surgeon, is very much an aside to the original purpose of their discussion, and the way they talk about it is as though it is a very strange event that has no explanation. Two highly respected medical professionals going on the record in a completely authentic way.

DR CHRIS YERINGTON'S CASE:

This is another case of a physician providing a report of an OBE almost as an aside. It was in response to a question that had been put to him: "As an anaesthesiologist, what has been your strangest experience while trying to put someone under." This is possibly the most astonishing verified OBE of all.

Circumstances: A patient referred to as Frank arrived at Ohio State University Hospital sometime late 2003, early 2004, with vital signs so bad he was effectively DOA. After placing Frank into hypothermic CA for a long period, he was wheeled into ICU where he was expected to die. Dr Yerrington returned to the hospital a day or so later to find that Frank had staged a full recovery. The 2 criteria:

1. Frank recognised Dr Yerington and told him about his OBE where he had witnessed the attempts to save his life, and noted something especially striking. He had been stuck on the ceiling for a long time and read and memorised the serial numbers on 3 lights in the OR. He also recalled conversations that occurred.

2. Dr Yerington confirmed that the conversations had happened during a period when Frank's EEG was isoelectric (flatline EEG). It was not possible for him to have heard these conversations. Most astonishing of all was the fact that the serial numbers were correct.

FLAPPING SURGEON

In this case a patient reported seeing an unusual activity while having an OBE.

Circumstances: Al Sullivan was undergoing surgery due to a heart problem in Hartford Hospital. During the surgery he had an OBE. The two criteria were met as follows:

1. As soon as Mr Sullivan was able to speak he told his cardiologist, Dr Anthony LaSala, about his OBE in which he saw a doctor standing over his body flapping his arms as though he were trying to take off.

2. Dr LaSala was taken aback by this account as Mr Sullivan's eyes had been taped shut during the operation, there was a drape between his head and the open chest cavity in which the surgeon was operating and given the stage of the operation that Sullivan noted the arm flapping he was almost certainly unconscious. The surgeon, Hiroyoshi Takata, was known for using his elbows to gesture to others what he

wanted to do and held his arms like wings when he did so. Takata, who seemed a bit defensive about the observations by the patient, would not confirm whether or not he did this during Mr Sullivan's operation but that it was something he did routinely. There were other details reported by Sullivan that were confirmed by Dr. LaSala, and were things he couldn't possibly have known.

MARIA'S TENNIS SHOE

This is probably the most famous verified OBE as it was one of the first to be publicly discussed as it was presented by Kenneth Ring, one of the founding fathers of NDE research. This occurred in 1979 in a Harbourview Hospital in Seattle.

Circumstances: Maria, a Spanish speaking migrant worker had a CA after being admitted into hospital a couple of days earlier. She then reported details from her OBE which fulfil the two criteria:

1. Maria told a social worker in the hospital, Kimberly Clark Sharp, about her OBE, and asked Sharp to see if there was a blue tennis shoe on a window ledge of the hospital a few floors off the ground.
2. Sharp investigated and found the shoe exactly how Maria described it. She concluded that the only way that Maria could have seen this was if she had indeed had an OBE. Various attempts to debunk this account have been made over the years, but none really hold water and say more about the character of the accusers than of the people involved.

THE 1985 QUARTER

Circumstances: An 82 year old patient called Ricardo was admitted to a hospital in San Antonio, Texas, after collapsing. He had a CA in hospital but responded to resuscitation by Dr. John Lerma. Once he was stabilised and fully conscious in the ICU he was very eager to talk to Dr Lerma about his OBE, and to confirm to himself that it had been real.

1. The patient told him various aspects of his NDE, and OBE but specifically said that there was a 1985 quarter on the top of a dusty high cabinet in the trauma room. He asked Lerma to check if it was there as he wanted to know that the amazing experience, including the beautiful aspects of his NDE, were indeed real.

2. Dr Lerma, in the presence of a couple of nurses got a ladder and looked on top of the cabinet and found the dusty quarter, which was indeed dated 1985. This experience had such an impact on Dr Lerma that he chose to pursue a career in end of life hospice medicine.

ANOTHER SERIAL NUMBER

Circumstances: At a hospital in New Jersey, a patient was admitted to a neurological unit in a coma. During her time there she had a CA and was resuscitated. When she came out of her coma, the patient told a nurse that she had an NDE and that she also had an OBE.

1. The patient told nurse Norma Bowe, who is now a PhD. Professor at Kean University, that she had OCD with a fixation for remembering numbers, and that she had memorised the serial number on top of a

7 foot respirator which stood by her bed. Nurse Bowe made a note of the serial number.

2. A few days later a technician came to remove the respirator because it was no longer needed. The nurse asked the technician to check if there was a serial number on the top. He did and it exactly matched the number that the patient had given.

There are more, so many more that endless books are filled with them. I have chosen these 7 because they share similar characteristics, namely the 2 criteria: a patient reporting seeing something specific during an OBE and an HCP confirming what was observed and, ideally, saying it was impossible for the patient to have made the observations through natural means.

What is so different from these 7 cases (along with hundreds of others which are similar) and the following:

Circumstances: A patient is admitted to New York Langone Medical Centre after collapsing with chest pain while shopping. The patient has a CA, but is resuscitated and makes a full recovery. Two weeks later the patient is contacted by a researcher at the hospital who asks them if they had any experiences.

1. The patient says they did but felt embarrassed about sharing it with the doctors who were very busy, but she remembered something she had seen while having an OBE. She had been above her body as the medical staff worked to resuscitate her and she saw a screen facing the ceiling with a picture of a fruit on it.

2. The researcher returns to NYU Langone where he reports the patient interview to the research team. He did not know what was projected at the time as he was blinded to this, but the researchers check the time of the CPR on this patient and what the iPad was supposedly showing on the screen, and it was indeed the same fruit.

Again, I ask what is so different from the 7 cases I described, and this case which would obviously be one that might eventually occur and be reported within the AWARE II study? Other than being part of a prospective study, in which the patients and staff were formally blinded to what the objects might be, this is essentially the same as the seven cases described. A patient reports seeing something specific and verifiable during an OBE to an HCP, the HCP checks that the observation was correct and that there is no way the patient could have seen this naturally. Fruit, or quarter, or serial number, or brain saw…there is no difference.

The real issue here is that the wider academic community which is strongly attached to a materialistic worldview, chooses to suggest that the highly trained HCPs with careers in medicine were either fools or liars.

I choose to look at the facts which are:

- Thousands of OBEs have been verified over the years.
- The vast majority of these OBEs were reported by ordinary people who had just experienced severe trauma, and nothing to gain from sharing what they believe had happened to them (as evidenced by the fact that their details are often not shared). To suggest that these thousands of patients imagined accurate details or were masters of illusion that make Penn and Teller look amateurs is absurd.
- Many hundreds of OBEs have been verified by highly professional HCPs, and sometimes by pre-eminent physicians who have been leaders in their field.

- These HCPs are often sceptical by nature, to suggest they were so easily fooled is an insult to their considerable intelligence and says more about the person making the suggestion than anything else.
- The only other alternative is that hundreds of HCPs across the world decided to lie in order to propagate a belief that the consciousness is able to survive death.

The fact is that it requires either a huge leap of imagination/delusion or a degree of materialistic stubbornness that makes a mule look compliant, to believe that either of the last two explanations is remotely plausible. But let's humour those who still might choose not to believe the mountain of evidence that exists.

Let's look at the evidence against NDEs and OBEs being real:

WHAT IS THE CURRENT SUM OF EVIDENCE AGAINST OBES BEING REAL?

Skeptics cite a number of scientific studies or observations to discredit the idea that OBEs and NDEs are real. These can be divided into two categories:

1. The patients' experiences were the result of some internal process arising from the brain's last firings after the heart stopped or due to CPR:

   ⊙ EEG signals have been observed in rats up to 30 seconds after CA[22][23] and in a small number of human subjects immediately prior to CA when life support was withdrawn.[24][25][26] While there were brief bursts of activity that may have been indicative of consciousness, in none of these cases was an NDE or OBE reported that could be correlated with this EEG activity, therefore any conclusions drawn or assertions made are based on speculation. In fact, I would go so far as to say that the claim made by Borjigin that the patients had EEG

---

22   Borjigin J, Lee U, Liu T, et al. Surge of neurophysiological coherence and connectivity in the dying brain. *Proc Natl Acad Sci U S A*. 2013;110(35):14432–14437.

23   Séverine Mahon, et al. Laminar organization of neocortical activities during systemic anoxia; Neurobiology of Disease; Volume 188, 2023, https://doi.org/10.1016/j.nbd.2023.106345

24   Electroencephalographic Recordings During Withdrawal of Life-Sustaining Therapy Until 30 Minutes After Declaration of Death; Norton, l et al; Can J Neurol Sci. 2017; 44: 139–145.

25   Enhanced Interplay of Neuronal Coherence and Coupling in the Dying Human Brain; Zemmar et al; Front. Aging Neurosci., 22 February 2022.

26   Borjigin J et al; Surge of neurophysiological coupling and connectivity of gamma oscillations in the dying human brain. PNAS 2023 May 9;120(19):e2216268120. doi: 10.1073/pnas.2216268120.

associated with consciousness during CA is false since the data from the human study only shows activity prior to CA.

⊚ The data from the AWARE II publication suggests that in a small number of patients, CPR can produce sufficient EEG activity to suggest consciousness may be present, but this has not so far been correlated with any accounts from the AWARE study. While this might appear to point to the theoretical possibility that conscious activity occurred, and therefore might provide succor to skeptics' claims that the brain is producing NDEs, as I explained in the previous section, there is no association therefore such suggestions are pure speculation.

It is absolutely fundamental to understand that there is no evidence from any study published to date (April 2025), whether it be in animals or humans, that brain activity around the time of death and reports of NDEs are associated. To date there has not been a single report of an NDE with accompanying EEG activity. You may have heard of the expression, association is not causation, well here there is not even any association, let alone there being a jot of evidence of causation. To this latter point, even if someone who had reported an NDE had EEG activity associated with it, the cause of this association is still a matter of speculation. It could be the "consciousness packing its bags and leaving" - the dis-inhibition/ disassociation hypothesis mentioned before, or it could be that the recollection of an NDE is indeed caused by brain activity, as suggested by materialists.

2. The conscious experiences described in NDE reports were induced by drugs administered to the patient which created images related to the patient's last conscious memories. For example, being in the ER.

    ⊚   Experiments using the kinds of drugs used in an ER in patients who are not having a CA have not been associated with NDE reports. However, NDE-like experiences, as well as OBEs, have been associated with the use of some psychedelic drugs; electrical stimulations of the brain; epileptic fits; or certain religious meditation techniques. Since none of these patients were dead, it could be argued that OBEs are not unique to NDEs.

Do either of these explanations—or any others—discredit the idea that NDEs or OBEs are real? No. Firstly, any reports of OBEs in other circumstances were not validated. Secondly, if they were, this might show that consciousness is able to momentarily separate itself from the body as a result of pharmacological, electrical, or neurological interference. If anything, such reports would reinforce the argument that the consciousness is a separate entity to the body and that the body is only a "host." However, unlike NDEs, what these other experiences do not demonstrate is that consciousness can survive death. Finally, while there may be instances that create passing residual brain activity, the simple fact is that a verified OBE in which a patient observed events that they could not have seen or heard because it was physically impossible (their eyes were closed or they had headphones on) are completely inexplicable using "natural explanations".

Some skeptics argue that the AWARE studies themselves are evidence that OBEs and NDEs are not real because they failed to produce a scientifically verified result. I hope by now it is obvious from the preceding sections that it is very clear why neither of the AWARE studies were likely to produce many, if any, scientifically validated visual OBEs. Quite simply the inclusion criteria for the studies were not focused on recruiting sufficient patients to reach the necessary interview stages to make it even remotely likely that a visual OBE would be verified. Such a study would need to follow tens of thousands of CA patients because so many of them fail to survive. There are only so many crash carts with iPads, oximetry equipment and personnel trained to use them that a team like Dr Parnia's can have. If more hospitals took part, and the inclusion criteria were changed, then AWARE II may well produce scientifically verified visual OBEs, as well as auditory OBEs.

In summary, a lack of a scientifically verified positive result is not evidence of a negative result, and in the absence of strong evidence to show that OBEs are indeed the product of a misfiring brain or drugs, the only conclusion to be drawn about evidence against OBEs being real is that there is none. None.

Related to this is the well-established fact that no one has ever provided a validated theory or scientific explanation of how the brain might generate consciousness. It is often referred to as one of the last remaining mysteries of science. It is merely a materialist assumption that the brain produces consciousness based on materialistic beliefs …namely that there is no such thing as the "soul" or "God" and that every observation has a physical or natural explanation. This is absolutely an assumption and not based on evidence. It is in fact just as scientific to postulate that consciousness is a separate entity to the brain as it is to postulate it is produced by the brain, but only if you ignore the evidence presented previously. Indeed, if you remove your own bias, when you consider the fact that there is no evidence or viable working theories that account for how the brain would produce consciousness, it is perfectly rational to hold the belief that the brain simply hosts consciousness.

If you then add in the sum total of evidence supporting the case for

OBEs being real, and no evidence against them being real, then it becomes far more rational to understand that consciousness is a separate entity from the brain.

WHY I PUBLISHED BEFORE A SCIENTIFICALLY VERIFIED OBE HAD BEEN CONFIRMED IN A PEER REVIEWED JOURNAL

Despite baseless assertions to the contrary from hardened skeptics, we have reached a point where OBEs have been shown to be real beyond reasonable doubt. This view is enforced by Dr. Parnia and other researchers in this field stating that the consciousness survives death. For example he said precisely that to a group of fellow physicians and scientists in December 2019 immediately after the AHA conference in which he presented the above data from AWARE II. He also says it in a podcast by resuscitation physicians in December 2020. This a serious clinical researcher, an expert on the medicine of bringing people back to life, who is highly regarded in the medical community, making concrete statements on the nature of consciousness to his peers. From the research he has conducted, he clearly has absolutely no doubt the phenomenon of OBEs is real. He has seen conclusive evidence. He states that consciousness survives the death of the body and is able to exist and "be conscious" for a period of time when the body is completely incapable of "producing" consciousness. Moreover, many other ER physicians state as much. They are utterly convinced, and these are also serious, highly credible and intelligent individuals who would know better than anyone else. They are not people who would risk their reputations endorsing half-baked unproven nonsense.

For personal subjective reasons, I admit I have been somewhat biased toward believing that NDEs are a real phenomenon. However, I am convinced we have now reached a tipping point of certainty and that is why I have published this book now rather than waiting for what could be many years before more data emerges. In my opinion, we have overwhelming evidence to support the understanding that the consciousness is a separate entity from the brain, and it does indeed persist beyond death. To believe otherwise is to believe that not only is Dr Parnia either a liar, or deluded, or completely incapable of processing observational and scientific information in a rational manner, but so too are hundreds, if not thousands of other doctors who also have stories from the ER or ICU that they cannot explain except in the terms of OBEs being real.

I have been sitting on a book like this for many years. The reason I have been waiting is that I felt the sum of evidence for and against the understanding that consciousness was a separate entity from the body, and capable of surviving death, had been balanced. However, I believe that my bias as a physical scientist who relies on laboratory equipment to conduct experiments has caused me to place a disproportionate amount of weight on having a "scientifically verified" OBE. The fact is that we have countless "professionally" verified OBEs, 7 of which I presented earlier. To discount these as being inferior in terms of believability to an OBE verified by an iPad is quite simply bonkers. In my view the totality of evidence proves beyond reasonable doubt that the OBE is a real phenomenon, therefore NDEs are as well, which means that the soul persists beyond death, at least for a short time, and therefore we should be entering a post materialistic era. It requires open discussion, like in this book, and others, for that era to be ushered in so that our collective understanding of what constitutes the meaning of life can be advanced, and as a result our individual lives and society as a whole can begin to benefit.

Scientific materialism, and its accompanying belief system of atheism, is a meme that is deadly to the human soul, and understanding that there is indeed a part of us that may be eternal, is vital to curing humanity from this harmful thought virus.

Skeptics argue that we need more data. What they are really saying is that they need more scientifically verified data because they don't believe thousands of doctors. We already have lots of data. We have thousands of verified anecdotal reports of OBEs from credible humans including healthcare professionals. We also have verified reports of OBEs observed by research scientists, in professional research settings. I don't know about you, but an iPad telling me it happened isn't going to make it any more compelling. Therefore, I believe that I show in this short book that we have enough evidence now to make an informed decision and that it would be wrong to delay my publishing this book any longer, just as it would be wrong for a physician to withhold a potentially life-saving drug from a patient with a terminal disease just because there were only a couple of studies showing it worked. While this analogy may seem somewhat hyperbolic, the truth, as we shall see before long, is that it is entirely appropriate since evidence from NDE data suggests that the "life of our souls" may indeed be in peril.

CHAPTER 4

WHAT DO THE NDE RESULTS MEAN?

Having reached our first destination of learning that the evidence proves OBEs are real, the gates are now open to a whole realm of implied possibilities. We will now travel through that realm, considering each of these possibilities in turn.

If you will recall, there are two possible hypotheses related to the AWARE studies that were not included by Dr. Parnia but are nonetheless useful for understanding the meaning of the results. As I've shown, it has been proven that when people's hearts stop beating, a small percentage of them are able to observe themselves and events outside of their body. This proves the first hypothesis to be true: *OBEs are a result of the consciousness persisting after the heart has stopped beating and brain activity has ceased. It therefore follows that the consciousness is a separate entity from the body, independent of brain function, and is able to survive death for an indeterminate period.*

What does this proof of the reality of OBEs mean for humanity, in particular, the existence of the soul? It means everything.

THE EXISTENCE OF THE SOUL

It is important to note that while the data we have proves the existence of a soul that is able to separate from the brain, it does not prove the existence of an *eternal* soul, something I touched on in the introduction. The conclusions drawn from the data on validated NDEs relate only to the period of time that the patient was clinically dead. The studies do not and cannot prove anything beyond that. However, I will speculate on what the data infers regarding the existence of an eternal soul. This discussion will have both evidence-based and philosophical elements to it.

Some may argue that this "floating" consciousness is some sort of quantum hangover from the brain's life and would stop existing at some point, but that is pure speculation with no evidence to support it. It may be true that the mechanisms of consciousness are somehow connected to quantum mechanics—for example, subatomic processes may enable the consciousness to exist in and interact with the tangible physical dimension—but that provides no evidence pointing to the origin of this consciousness or its ability to persist indefinitely. If the consciousness uses quantum mechanics to interact with the brain, it doesn't necessarily imply that the brain generates it.

The evidence for the belief that consciousness persists much longer than the duration of the NDE does not lie in science but rather in the thousands of different belief systems that have evolved over the millennia that state the soul is eternal. Various prophets have said so in one form or another, some of whom were very specific about the eternal nature of a person's soul, including the one I follow, Jesus Christ. Many tribal belief systems maintain that their ancestors exist as "spirits." In addition, some NDErs report that they are told by beings they meet during their NDEs, that the soul is eternal and will persist forever.

In isolation, these pieces of "evidence" don't amount to anything more than subjective beliefs, but when combined with the clear proof that the consciousness is independent of the body and is able to exist beyond death, these subjective reports and "understandings" need to be taken more seriously. They both corroborate and are corroborated by the totality of data from validated OBEs. It is now rational and scientifically consistent to believe that our consciousness has the potential to be eternal.

This is the first and most important "so what" to come out of the findings of the AWARE studies.

However, that is just the beginning since we now have strong supporting evidence for the second hypothesis: *If OBEs are proven to be real, then so too, by inference, are other core elements of NDEs.*

THE OTHER CORE ELEMENTS

Because OBEs have been validated, and therefore people's reports of OBEs are true, it follows that their other reported experiences are also likely to be true observations rather than just random output from a poorly functioning brain. If the OBE is not the result of a physiological process, then wouldn't the same apply to all other aspects of NDEs? This line of extrapolative thinking is supported by the fact that there is a multitude of similar accounts with the same core experiences from all age groups and backgrounds. It could be argued that if the other core elements were generated by chemical or electrical events in a dying brain or from experiencing pulses of oxygenated blood via CPR, then they should be much more random in nature. They are not. The accounts are reproducible across all demographics, and the sequence of events reported in NDEs always seems to follow a logical and consistent timeline.

So what are these other core elements? They are the other nine components of the Greyson scale for measuring whether conscious recollections reported from CA survivors are classified as NDEs or not. Since the RED elements described in the recent consensus statement are relatively new, and include too many sub elements to describe here, I will stick with the Greyson scale that does a very good job of capturing the most familiar NDE elements.:

1. Awareness of being dead
2. Intense emotions, most commonly of profound peace, well-being, and love; others marked by fear, horror, and loss
3. Rapidly moving through darkness or a tunnel, often toward an indescribable light
4. Incredibly rapid, sharp thoughts and observations
5. A sense of being "somewhere else," in a landscape that seems like a spiritual realm or world (I prefer and use the word dimension)
6. Encounter with deceased loved ones, sacred figures or unrecognized beings which are consoling, loving, or terrifying
7. A life review by reliving actions and feeling their emotional impact on others
8. A boundary that represents a decision to return to the body or to stay
9. Communication with a Supreme Being of Light, or just light

Let's break these down for a brief closer look (if you wish to review numerous more detailed accounts there are many books on NDEs documenting multiple experiences. *After* by Bruce Greyson and *The Self Does Not Die* By Titus Rivas would be a good starting point).

AWARENESS OF BEING DEAD:

This is self-explanatory. People having an OBE with an awareness of being dead often describe looking at their dead body and feeling nothing. Occasionally they might be sad or afraid, but the most common emotional response to the sight of their dead bodies is indifference. Perhaps if we realized that our consciousness survived beyond the death of our bodies, we might not think that the death of our bodies is as horrible as we believe it to be while physically alive. Our desperate need to cling to physical life may, for a moment, be removed and our body might become almost anachronistic, even an encumbrance. Many describe the return to their bodies as unpleasant, confining, and even disappointing.

INTENSE EMOTIONS, MOST COMMONLY OF PROFOUND PEACE, WELL-BEING, AND LOVE; OTHERS MARKED BY FEAR, HORROR, AND LOSS:

Once the consciousness has left their body, some people report feeling intense emotions. The one most often described is an overwhelming sense of peace; an assurance that everything will be alright. Also, people report experiencing love with an intensity greater than they ever experienced in this life. Others, thankfully in the minority, have extremely negative emotions marked by fear or even horror.

RAPIDLY MOVING THROUGH DARKNESS OR A TUNNEL, OFTEN TOWARD AN INDESCRIBABLE LIGHT:

After an OBE, many NDErs describe passing through a tunnel of some sort, often at an incredible speed and accompanied by the sound of wind and the sense of passing through time and space. Often there is a light at the end of the tunnel—a light they are drawn to.

I won't go into discussions often cited about physiological explanations of the tunnel involving the last signals from the retina. Right now we are working on the assumption that because the OBE has been proven to be real, all other reports of core elements by extrapolation are reports of events that occurred while the patient is clinically dead.

So, what does this tunnel represent? Since it often precedes NDErs encountering dead relatives, a "being of light," and seeing visions of beautiful dimensions, it would not be unreasonable to believe this is a passage between the universe in which we live—one that is dominated by the rules of physics and time—and somewhere else. Or perhaps it could be a connection to another place within this universe. Either is complete conjecture, but it is reported as a journey of infinite length and time, as though there is a clear demarcation between two different dimensions

INCREDIBLY RAPID, SHARP THOUGHTS AND OBSERVATIONS:

In OBEs, on both sides of the "tunnel," people often describe all their senses as being enhanced. For example, they describe having 360-degree vision. Also, their speed of understanding and other aspects of cognition is accelerated. Answers to deep mysteries are suddenly understood with no effort of thought. Earlier I touched on the question of how one can experience the use of physical senses during an OBE when their physical sensors are still on a gurney. In the appendix, I will discuss this in much more depth.

A SENSE OF BEING "SOMEWHERE ELSE," IN A LANDSCAPE THAT SEEMS LIKE A SPIRITUAL REALM OR WORLD:

In my father's NDE, he found himself in a meadow surrounded by flowers that were beautiful beyond imagination with colors he had never before seen. This is a quite common report from NDEs. People from a Christian western culture will usually describe this "realm" as heaven.

If you are a materialist, you may consider this nonsense, but remember, the OBE has been proven real. As the OBE is real, heaven is also real.

For people of faith, all of this makes complete sense and is even exciting—it confirms what they already believe. Skeptics and materialists may not agree. However, if such a place as heaven exists, and what people have reported is indeed that place, then heaven is not in the clouds or air but beyond the confines of understood reality.

Also, it is important to note that while NDErs describe these experiences as being beyond the ability of human terminology to express, it is also true to say that no single subjective account of the landscapes, forms, buildings or vistas observed in these realms is the same as another. There is huge variability and while they all describe these places as feeling more real than life here, and as being their real home, the fact they are all different does leave some unanswered questions.

I am latterly of the view that this variability is not solely due to subjective interpretation of what the experiencers observed, but something more fundamental related to the importance of free will. This fresh understanding is central to my discussions in the book: *Did Jesus Die For Nothing? The evidence from Near Death Experiences.*

ENCOUNTER WITH DECEASED LOVED ONES, SACRED FIGURES, OR UNRECOGNIZED BEINGS:

Many NDErs describe meeting relatives or occasionally friends (and even pets) whom they were close to during their lives. The NDErs are often welcomed. Sometimes they sense others whom they didn't know. They are described as guardian angels or "spirit guides." This has often been reported in accounts by reliable NDErs. What the spirit guides are and what role they have is completely open to interpretation. While there is strong correlation across different incidences, the perceptions and understandings of what the NDErs experience are subjective. However, the sheer numbers of these experiences suggest that it's true and that some of us can expect to experience the same at our time of death.

A LIFE REVIEW:

Countless NDErs report the experience of seeing their whole life, every minute detail, and being invited to reflect on all their actions and the impacts those actions had on those around them. It is an objective analysis guided by a "celestial" being, or beings, covering what went well and what did not. They also get to experience their behavior from other people's viewpoints, specifically to show how their actions made others feel.

Almost as an aside, I want to mention my favorite NDE account … Howard Storm experienced a remarkable NDE that turned his life in a completely different direction—a reasonably common outcome. He went from being an atheist Christian-bashing university professor to a Baptist minister. His NDE is famous for many things, some of which I will return to, but what really struck me was his account of his life review. Howard Storm had been an academic and an accomplished sportsman. He had obviously been someone driven to succeed, but when he experienced his life review with "other beings," the piece of his life they got the most excited about—and which got the highest "approval ratings"—was the night when, as a teenager, he heard his sister crying in a neighboring bedroom and went in to hug and comfort her for the rest of the night. This appeared to be one of the most important things he did in his entire life.

This points to a common component that comes from virtually all NDEs: Life is about many things, but most of all it is about loving others. According to many NDErs, our primary purpose in life is to love.

A BOUNDARY THAT REPRESENTS A DECISION TO RETURN TO THE BODY OR TO STAY:

Many NDErs report a point in their experience where they are told, or are aware, that if they go any farther into this new dimension, they can never come back. Alternatively, sometimes, even if they want to stay—as is often the case because the experience can be beautiful—they are told they must return, as they haven't completed their purpose in life. In the past I have shrugged at this core element, barely giving it a second thought, but as my views on NDEs have evolved with time I have come to believe that the existence of this boundary is highly relevant to how we should interpret what NDErs report from these dimensions. My thoughts on what the boundary represents, like certain other facets that I avoid exploring in this book, inevitably lead to subjective and disputable interpretations based on one's own worldview. As a result, and to avoid the unpleasant sense that the reader is being subjected to religious bias, I have saved these discussions for my book *Did Jesus Die For Nothing?*

Now we come to the last and possibly the most important core element: Communication with a supreme Being of Light, or just light.

THE BEING OF LIGHT

After meeting the people of light, the experiencer may meet a powerful spiritual being some have identified as God, Jesus, or some other religious figure. Identifying this being seems to be a function of one's religious background or training; there is a cultural component present. Experiencers have a strong sense of interconnectedness during the encounter. They may gain knowledge of future events and receive messages regarding life's purpose, although they have difficulty verbalizing this afterwards. Regardless of their prior beliefs, whether

agnostic, somewhat skeptical or deeply religious, most of these people
are convinced that they had been in the presence of some supreme and
loving power and were given a brief glimpse of a life yet to come.[27]

The above is a quote from one of many websites on NDEs and expresses a common theme: in spite of cultural interpretations of who the being is, the Being of Light is universally described as a being of immense loving power.

For me, *the most* significant core element of the NDE is this Being of Light. This experience, more than any other, can be the most transformative. It alters perspective forever and puts into context the daily squabbles over money, work, and power. After this encounter, the experiencer is left with no doubt that it is the Being of Light's desire for us to live our lives as loving beings. The message seems to be that there is never any excuse for taking another human life, especially for the sake of imposing a religion or ideology on others. In addition, the pursuit of material possessions, power, or recognition is a dangerous distraction from our primary purpose, which is to love. Feedback from NDErs who claim to have communicated with the Being of Light or other spiritual beings on the other side share a consistent message: Life is about two things: First and most importantly, it is about loving. Secondly, it is about learning. Some NDErs describe earth as a school, and that it is one of the toughest.

EVIDENCE FOR THE EXISTENCE OF GOD

EVIDENCE FROM NDES

Now I'd like to return to the second part of the question I pose on the cover of this book and in the first chapter, specifically that the data from accounts of,

27   Foundation for near death experiences: http://neardeathfoundation.org/near_death_experience.asp.

and studies on NDEs prove that God exists. Since the OBE has been proved real, is it right to infer that the Being of Light is real too?

The Being of Light described here does not sound like the God described by some of the prophets in the Bible or other religious texts. Howard Storm recounts how, during his NDE, while he met beings of light, who he described as guides, he didn't meet the main Being of Light but saw it from a distance, as though it were the center of a galaxy. To Storm, it was unapproachable because he was so ashamed of his own lack of goodness compared to the light.

While the accounts of NDErs do not completely align with the understanding of God shaped by some religions, I believe these reports should convince everyone that a God of some sort exists, and from numerous accounts from otherwise reliable people, this God is a Being of such immense love that to describe standing in his/her/its/their presence is impossible.

Until recently, the secular establishment supported by vocal atheist scientists has dismissed beliefs in the idea of a consciousness that survives death as nonsense, but now there are sufficient validated reports of OBEs which show consciousness persists outside of the body for at least the first moments or even minutes after death. These same OBE reports include other elements of the NDE as described above, with many describing the Being of Light. Since their reports of OBEs have been validated, by extrapolation, so, too, is the existence of a Being of Light, or God.

For some people this is a step too far—even an affront—but for others who haven't had an NDE but have experienced this Being through faith, it is not news and yet in some ways it is. Faith has always been about believing in something you cannot see or prove to be true, but that is changing. Religious belief may become just a little less about faith and a bit more about rational deduction.

Is there any other evidence that God exists?

HUMAN TESTIMONY

Throughout history we have relied on human testimony to make decisions on a subject, whether it be in a court of law, reports by explorers of strange animals, or journalists reporting an event, and so on. Prior to the invention of modern technologies, truth was determined through human observation, discussion, and reason. Now it seems few of us trust anyone but their closest friends or family members. The proliferation of fake news and deep divisions in our society make discourse on just about any subject a social minefield, with claims and counter claims founded on myths and lies.

Unless there is a photo or a proven experiment to support a claim, many of us are inclined to dismiss events. Even when there is strong evidence, we will still dismiss it if it challenges our fundamental worldview. This has been confirmed through numerous psychological experiments. One researcher wrote:

> *Someone with a conviction is a hard person to change. Tell them you disagree, and they turn away. Show them facts or figures and they question your sources. Appeal to logic and they fail to see your point. …Suppose that they are presented with evidence, unequivocal and undeniable evidence, that their belief is wrong: what will happen? The individual will frequently emerge, not only unshaken, but even more convinced of the truth of their beliefs than ever before.*[28]

Skeptics have chosen to dismiss the accounts of thousands of respectable individuals regarding NDEs and OBEs. However if thousands of respectable, credible men and women described specific instances in which a famous politician or celebrity had groped women, a court would regard this as extremely strong evidence, even proof. Similarly, materialist skeptics such as

---

28   Leon Festinger, Henry Riecken, and Stanley Schacter: When Prophecy Fails, 1957

evolutionist Richard Dawkins have also ignored billions of people regarding religious faith. This is despite the fact that for thousands of years people from all over the world have reported encounters with God or gods of various names, which provides very strong supporting evidence for his/her/its/their existence, especially when combined with the now verified encounters from NDEs.

Skeptics, however, dismiss belief in God as a meme—a thought virus passed down from one generation to another—and discount all mystical experiences of God as a delusion, a lie, or a hallucination. Just as with NDEs, to completely dismiss human testimony without strong opposing evidence, is definitely subjective, possibly arrogant, but most of all it is not scientific or rational. There is one piece of evidence from science to support the existence of God that cannot be ignored but often is, and that is the fact that there is no evidence to support the belief that life might have spontaneously appeared by natural means and a significant piece of evidence supporting an "intelligent" origin.

DNA AND THE "ORIGIN OF LIFE" QUESTION

DNA and the origin of life conundrum provides further supporting evidence for the existence of God. I'll summarize here the key conclusions from the book I published on this topic in 2019 titled *DNA: The Elephant in the Lab.* I provide a more in depth summary of the major themes from that book in the appendix of this book. These conclusions are not just my own, although having a Ph.D. in organic chemistry and having spent much of my career becoming intimate with the biochemistry behind protein synthesis and cellular replication, I am reasonably well qualified to comment on the subject. However, if it was just me who was drawing these conclusions, I would hesitate to assert them publicly, but it is not, and there are many others, including eminent atheist scientists who are deeply troubled by the questions surrounding how life came into being. Why?

In general, the modern scientific dogma only allows for natural explanations, and therefore it is assumed that the appearance of life on earth was the result of a natural process or event. However, and I will spare you the lengthy details here, this is the gist of the problem with this assumption:

- There is no evidence that life was the result of a natural process.
- There are no viable theories as to how life might have come into being by a natural process.
- There is significant, arguably insurmountable, evidence against life appearing as the result of a natural process. Here are four examples of the evidence:
  - ◉ No uncontrolled system, let alone the chaotic early earth environment, would be capable of producing sufficient quantities of pure starting materials to generate the complex biochemical constructs that would constitute the simplest conceivable life forms.
  - ◉ Even if there were unlimited quantities of starting materials, the odds against the spontaneous natural assembly of just one of these complex biochemical structures are so immense that we would need at the very least a multiverse of multiverses for it to have happened at one time point on any planet. In other words, it is statistically in the realms of fantasy.
  - ◉ The "chicken and egg" paradox of which came first, DNA or the proteins it codes for defies natural explanation, as evidenced by the fact that no one has provided an explanation that stands up to serious scrutiny.

⊚   The frozen nature of the DNA code and its translation machinery points to a system that is impossible to fiddle with, and does not evolve, nor could have evolved from a simpler system. Even the most credulous atheist scientists would not believe that this system could form spontaneously via a natural process.

This leaves atheist scientists in a bit of a spot, as they are forced to believe in a hypothesis that is shown to be impossible because they will not allow for anything other than a natural solution. They rightly rail against a "God of the gaps" solution, which argues that because we don't understand how it happened it must have been God. This is extremely unsatisfactory to any enquiring mind, but what if there was actual measurable evidence that DNA was the result of intelligence?

This is not intelligent design, which focuses on evolution, but specifically relates to the origin of DNA, which predates biological evolution. Again, I will spare you the details here, but the central premise is that DNA is proven by all definitions to be a code, and because all other codes are known only to have intelligent origins, and there is no viable alternative explanation, it is rational to conclude that the DNA code was also the result of intelligence.

In summary, you have no evidence for life appearing naturally, lots of evidence against it, and evidence for life being initiated by a Being of vast creative intelligence.

IS ALL THIS ACTUALLY PROOF THAT A GOD EXISTS?

Does the evidence I've presented thus far—scientific and non-scientific— prove the existence of God? The following are the three key pieces of evidence.

Let's review and decide.

1. The totality of evidence proves that OBEs—and therefore NDEs—are real, verifies the existence of the soul. Reports from NDEs indicate there is a Being of Light, or God. The NDE reports describe this being as a specific presence who is both infinitely loving and knowledgeable.
2. Myriad belief systems, many of which evolved independently of one another, point to "supreme spiritual beings" or gods, or a God. Many people who are alive today, including myself, believe and testify they have encountered this Being through their personal religious practice. Because these belief systems are derived from human reports over the millennia, they must be counted as additional evidence, no matter how highly or lowly you regard the quality of that evidence. Human testimony is evidence.
3. Very strong scientific evidence indicates that life was initiated by a being of unimaginable intelligence with the ability to manipulate chemical processes in a manner far in advance of any technology we have today. The existence of a DNA code is evidence of a "higher" intelligent being.

In isolation, none of these pieces of evidence "prove" that God exists. However, when combined, I believe they do prove beyond reasonable doubt that God does indeed exist.

CHAPTER 5

FURTHER IMPLICATIONS
FROM RESEARCH ON NDES

Research now provides evidence beyond reasonable doubt that human beings have souls that may be eternal and that a creative being with specific intelligence—God—exists. This either confirms your existing worldview or is immensely challenging to get your head around. Either way, the existence of the soul, or God, is just the beginning of what NDEs reveal to humanity and the destiny of the soul. What else can we learn from the reports of the afterlife from existing accounts? Specifically, what can we expect from an afterlife, and who can expect to have an afterlife?

It's an important question to consider. We have eighty to ninety years on this planet, if we're lucky, and then possibly eternity afterwards. Maybe the decisions we make and our behavior here on Earth have implications for what happens to our souls once our bodies have died.

DARK EXPERIENCES: IS THIS HELL?

First, I'm going to explore the possibility of dark experiences. According to historical accounts between 6 and 25 percent of reported NDEs describe going down a different road than the one that leads to a beautiful realm and the Being of Light. As is the case with all NDEs, these darker experiences may differ in specific details, but they usually share certain themes or elements.

In the recent consensus statement these experiences have been dismissed as not being true NDEs. Specifically, in the supplemental section the following statement is made:

"However, typically, these so called 'negative NDE' neither share the same narrative or themes as the classical NDE, nor do they share the same transcendent qualities, ineffability, and long-term transformative effects of the classical NDE. In sum, so called negative NDE appear to be fundamentally and phenomenologically different from the classical NDE. In reality, the majority of these descriptions largely represent a mislabeling of ICU delirium and delusions..."

This statement has a citation attached to it [A systematic analysis of distressing near-death experience accounts; Cassol et al.] This paper repeats a number of times that the only overall difference in terms of measurable elements of negative NDEs from classical NDEs, is that negative NDEs have a less positive affect, otherwise "distressing and classical accounts do not seem to differ regarding total score as well as on the three other components of the Greyson NDE scale (i.e. cognitive, paranormal and transcendental)."

In this paper 14% of people have negative NDEs, about half of whom have hellish NDEs, and the descriptions bare many similarities to classical NDEs, such as a tunnel, being hyper aware, timelessness, OBEs, 360 degree vision. I therefore believe that Dr Parnia and his colleagues are seriously mistaken to not categorize these as REDs or authentic NDEs. It may be well-meaning, but it is extremely dangerous, especially given the kinds of experience described and the implications:

One common theme is the presence of other extremely unpleasant beings. In Howard Storm's account of his NDE, he describes popping out of his body, and after frantically trying to get his wife to listen to him, but to no avail, he heard voices coming from beyond an open door in the corner of the hospital room. He decided to follow them since initially the voices surrounding him seemed friendly. But suddenly their demeanor changed, and even though he no longer had a physical body, they began to violate him. The pain felt real, and the fear was absolute. Fortunately, he escaped. Were those creatures demons or other tortured souls?

It's impossible to know, but there are many other accounts of people experiencing pain and suffering in their NDE and returning from the experience with a real fear of death. It is also possible this type of NDE is underreported because the people were ashamed, or embarrassed, or confused, or simply thought it was a form of nightmare. Either way it poses a very important question: is this place really hell?

This lady whose experience is recounted in the 2019 paper on negative NDEs states that it is:

"There are more and more entities surrounding me and this dark environment is unbearable. The deafening noise invades the space that becomes increasingly dark. I would like this noise to stop. I am caught in a whirlwind, the dark grey haze around me is thick, and the smell and sound are getting more unbearable [...]. And I am beginning to distinguish forms in this incredibly thick fog. Human, bestial, monstrous. I am swimming in a stinking stench filled with horrible and furtive creatures and I am feeling overwhelmed with pain. It hurts everywhere, no, worse, I am becoming pain. I understand that my suffering is just beginning. And I am scared. A growing fear, appalling. I would like to close my eyes and stop hearing and feeling. But it is impossible. My vision is very wide, I see everywhere at once, I see in front of me, above, below and on the sides; only a small part on the back is not visible. The less I want to hear, see and feel, the more receptive I am. It is terrible, it is like I am absorbing the pain and suffering of all these beings…I am extremely lucid, I feel aware like I have never been before. Time no longer exists. I wish I could escape this place, escape time, but my anguish is such that I cannot move…as if these beings were holding me back. […] I understand that I am between two worlds and that this in-between is none other than Hell". (Female, 42 years old)

Accounts like this should not be dismissed as readily as Dr Parnia does, and should serve as warnings that eternal joy is not guaranteed.

Another common dark theme reported by many NDErs is precisely just that, an experience of darkness. Not just any darkness, but a creeping, cold darkness that threatens to engulf them and from which they know there is no return. Is this hell or is it ultimate death—that is, the death of the soul—a topic I will return to later.

Are these dark experiences completely random, or is there some correlation between faith in God and/or "righteous" behavior in this life? There is very little available from the accounts to steer our thinking on this. Some who have had these dark experiences said they believed in God, and some who claim to have good experiences were atheists (though they rarely are afterwards).

The answers are not easily discerned from the accounts, and I personally fall back on what my faith tells me about this subject. Others might be left somewhat baffled by it. However, what is certain is that there is clear direction for how we should best live our lives according to those who claim to have communicated with the Being of Light.

To complicate matters, a small percentage of NDEs report learning of reincarnation as a step toward spiritual development. If one hasn't learned what they were supposed to in one life, they may have an opportunity to live another life, so they are ready to move on to the spiritual dimension and not go back.

This is controversial for people of my faith, and given the small numbers that make this claim, perhaps we shouldn't put too much stock in the belief that we'll get to have another life after this one if we get it wrong now.[29]

For many, the notion of a Being of Light that's loving and forgiving yet creating or allowing the existence of hell—where humans would suffer "eternal torture"—creates a glaring inconsistency. How could such a loving Being allow this to happen? That is a huge question, and one that is outside of the scope of this text, but one that I cover in *Did Jesus Die For Nothing?*

Nevertheless, numerous NDE accounts indicate that a very dark experience awaits some people after they die. While those who have not been exposed to any of the world's theistic religions might find this offensive, to those who do have faith in God, particularly those who subscribe to one of the Abrahamic faiths, the concept of God's justice is nothing new, and some of us understand that our idea of justice is not always aligned with God's.

One thing to take into account, however, is that, according to NDE reports, it is possible that the dark state that we describe as hell, isn't eternal. Howard Storm's experience wasn't permanent; he is one of many who report escaping a state of torment and entering a heavenly realm. Even though he returned from his NDE back to life, one can't help but ask what happens to those who enter the dark state and stay dead? There is so much that is unknown. We are getting only glimpses into a vast mystery.

---

29 My personal view is that whatever the truth of the matter is on reincarnation, why take the chance that you will have another go at life? When we are told by religious figures and the NDE experiencers how we should behave in this life, why ignore them in the belief that we *might* get another go? What I mean is that if you don't make the most of this life, and then find out upon your death that there is no reincarnation or you've blown your "allocation" of lives, then that would be the end—no new life, no eternal life, no cake, no cigar, and possibly something worse, if the likes of Howard Storm are to be believed: hell.

STATE OF LIMBO

Some NDErs, report entering a state of limbo where they experience a "restless state of greyness."

Does this mean it's eternal?

PLACE OF LIGHT

Feedback from NDErs who claim to have communicated with the Being of Light or other spiritual beings on the other side share a consistent message: Life is about two things. First and most importantly, it is about loving. Secondly, it is about learning.

I hoped the afterlife would be something like this: access to all of space, time, people, their personal experiences, and ultimately, God—a "universal space/time library" of everything that has occurred everywhere forever. Imagine being able to go to any point in history and witness it in as much detail as possible. Imagine witnessing the birth of life on Earth or visiting galaxies that to us on Earth are merely pinpricks of light in the sky. Or what about standing in the presence of the Being of Light and feeling overwhelming, never-ending love?

Hardened materialists have returned from this alternative dimension of consciousness after an NDE with tales of having the ability to think of a place and time and not only be there but experience it in incredible detail. In that place of light, it's as though our current life is a story that has been written for all of us to experience in incredible detail after this life, forever. All of history is written in a living book that you can actually experience, with every detail perfectly recorded. In fact, it is possible that all that has happened in the universe is recorded for eternity for those who live forever and that they are then able to observe these events, and even experience them fully. You wouldn't need Netflix there!

In my father's NDE, after he hovered above his body, he found himself in a beautiful meadow. It was warm and the colors were more vivid than any he'd seen before. He sensed it wasn't a meadow that had ever existed in real life, but it felt just as real—maybe even more so. Many others have reported NDE experiences of places with unimaginable beauty full of life, color, and love.

How are all of these ideas—of heavenly realms, demon-infested darkness, grey voids, and even an archived universe—possible?

We know so little. We may have verified that the soul, or our consciousness, is an independent entity that experiences our current dimensions through occupying a physical body, but we can't conceive of what other dimensions—populated with unique landscapes and beings— there might be. What lies on the other side of this life may be so much better than we can possibly begin to imagine.

Isn't setting our sights on the possibility of God and heaven a worthy goal? Doesn't all this knowledge put into perspective the earthly, material things we crave and struggle for in our daily existence? I believe this lies at the heart of the question of how we avoid the darkness and reach the light.

CHAPTER 6

WHAT ABOUT THE TEN PERCENT?

Now we come onto what I believe is one of the most important, and possibly controversial aspects of NDEs, and a subject that seems to be largely skimmed over by other writers. It is this topic and the conclusions I have drawn which have caused me to go through the effort of writing this book.

In this section I add a new word that can be interchanged with soul or consciousness: spirit. This word has a religious association to it, which is why I have avoided it thus far, but it nonetheless describes the same entity I have been referring to throughout this book. Concepts such as spirituality are going to be covered in this section, and there are no equivalent words with the same meaning; it is necessary to introduce it.

I have described three types of outcome reported from many NDEs: the dark, the limbo, and the light. But there is one more possible outcome: death. By that I don't mean physical death, but something that I believe is far worse: spiritual death. There is a saying: "Fear not the one who can kill your body, rather fear him who can kill your soul."[30]

The idea of spiritual death—a concept embraced by some religions—is obviously entirely speculative in the context of the evidence that we have been discussing. It is just one of a number of hypothetical explanations for the factual observation that not everyone who is clinically dead and then achieves ROSC has an NDE. Moreover, my introduction of this notion is most likely a result of my faith, from which the above quote comes. Really much of this next section is me "thinking out loud." That doesn't mean it is wrong, but it is important to note that context.

According to recent literature, cardiac arrests (CA) with reports of NDEs ranges somewhere between 10 and 20 percent of people, most of whom were elderly. It begs the question, why doesn't everyone report NDEs since we now know they are a real phenomenon?

Three possibilities come to mind:

1. Eighty to ninety percent of people who have a CA don't report NDEs because, while they may have had one, they don't remember them.

2. Eighty to ninety percent of times that people have a CA, the consciousness does not become immediately "detached" from the brain …it stays where it is in an unconscious state.

3. Eighty to ninety percent of people who have a CA do not have an "eternal" soul or consciousness at the point of physical death—they have a consciousness suitable for existing in the physical world, but for some reason it is incapable of progressing to the "next dimension." One potential reason is that the part that was born eternal has become permanently "tethered" to the physical body that hosted it. Essentially, when the body dies, the soul will die with the flesh that hosts it.

---

30   This is actually from the gospel according to St Matthew, chap 10 vs 28 KJV. The full quote is even more troubling: "And fear not them which kill the body, but are not able to kill the soul: but rather fear him which is able to destroy both soul and body in hell."

Now let's break these down into more detail …

1. WHY WOULD SOMEONE HAVE AN NDE AND NOT REMEMBER IT?

It has been suggested that all people dream every night, but many people do not remember their dreams. Therefore, in the same way that people do not always remember their dreams, it may be possible that, for similar reasons, all people who have a CA, also have an NDE, but not all people remember them.

This is perfectly plausible, and it is quite possibly the reason for the low number of NDE reports after CA. It is certainly the explanation I believe will be most popular, as it is the least controversial or disquieting. Dr. Parnia once subscribed to this idea when presenting an explanation for this phenomenon. He now focuses on pharmacological and physiological reasons. This may account for some of the memory loss, but given the huge differences in recollection between children and elderly adults, despite the use of the same methods (something I discuss in detail shortly), I do not believe that this explanation is satisfactory, not least because the data suggests that the brain is not working at all during these experiences, therefore these factors should not influence the laying down of memory...an issue I return to at the beginning of the appendix.

Another physiological reason cited for not remembering NDEs have been covered previously and include that the older the patient, the less likely they are to remember having one. This explanation might seem like common sense, but as I will discuss shortly, the data does not fully support this.

Another reason may be related to differing levels of innate spirituality. By this I mean that there could be physiological or psychological factors that inhibits their ability to navigate, interact with, or in this instance, remember events or encounters from this particular "dimension". An example along these lines makes me think of a time when I began dating a woman who did not profess having any faith, but because of mine, she started attending church with me. However, even after a long period of attending together, our experiences of church and prayer were quite different. Sometimes, particularly in corporate worship songs, I experience a strong sense of "God's presence." However, she never had a sense of God's presence, despite us both being exposed to the possibility in an identical environment. She desperately wanted it and would pray for it, but to no avail.

What could be the reason?

Perhaps the experience I and many other churchgoers have is fake— God does not exist and our experience of Him is an illusion. However, this scenario is less likely, considering what we have learned from the validation of OBEs and leaves two alternative explanations:

- She was unable to experience the presence of God directly, despite seeking it, because she did not have the "natural" sensory capacity; her psychology or physiology did not allow it.
- She could not experience God's presence because God is a "spiritual" being and she didn't have a sufficiently developed spirit/soul that was able to connect with or experience that dimension. [31]

In other words, either her physical equipment (brain) was inadequate, or her consciousness was inadequate.

So how could it be that one person has the natural sensory capacity in their brain to experience God and another doesn't?

During the early part of this century, researchers showed that spirituality may be a genetic trait. [32] This evidence is discussed in Dean Hamer's book

31   A being of an entirely different dimension outside of our own physical dimension.

32   Silveira, L A. "Experimenting with Spirituality: Analyzing the God Gene in Nonmajors Laboratory Course" CBE:Life Sciences Education. 7 (1):132–145.

The God Gene, where he reviewed evidence that a portion of our genetic code called VMAT2 is related to our propensity to be spiritual.

What if a portion of the brain is like a radio receiver, capable of interacting with or sensing the presence of beings from the spiritual dimension, including a Being such as God? If that were true, and some people's brains were better developed in this area, then they might be more spiritual as a result. Conversely, if spiritual people were weeded out of society over the past hundreds of years through religious persecution, it is possible that the VMAT2 gene has regressed and the general population has become less spiritual.

It is hard to see an evolutionary benefit to a spiritual gene if it does not deliver a physical survival advantage, therefore it should be equally present— or absent—in all humans. However, while it may be true that being more spiritual does not lend a survival advantage (and in fact may be a disadvantage because of persecution), it is possible that being less spiritual does lend a survival advantage. If one's primary focus in life is on material gain and success, which is regarded as being less spiritual, it possibly confers a survival advantage in our material existence and therefore people with these traits become genetically dominant. This is of course a can of worms and is totally speculative, so not worth exploring further in this text.

In conclusion about spiritual ability, it may be possible that some people are less able to perceive spiritual things and yet still have a spirit. It is possible that despite people losing that connection between their physical minds and the spiritual world and becoming spiritually "blind," a soul or a spirit still remains in that person. They may be isolated from the spiritual world and from God— which results in a lack of sensitivity in spiritual matters—but their status as spiritual beings is the same as those who are more developed spiritually.

Bringing this back to the subject at hand—memory of NDEs—a lack of spiritual awareness could also be linked to the ability to remember dreams or NDEs. The concepts might not seem connected, but all involve the consciousness either interacting with or existing in different (spiritual) dimensions—ones that we now know to exist because OBEs have been proven real. It is possible that just as some people don't remember dreams or don't experience any spiritual presence, neither do they remember NDEs.

Another potential reason why people cannot remember NDEs may be due to the frightening possibility that the experience was extremely traumatic. The specific term for this is dissociative amnesia. If, as mentioned previously, a small proportion of people report having a hell-like experience, maybe there are others for whom it was so horrific, their subconscious buries it so they can't relive the trauma again. Maybe, and I hope this isn't the case, hell-like NDEs are more common than reported because some of those poor souls that have them can't remember them due to dissociative amnesia. I appreciate this is a very controversial and disturbing suggestion, but nonetheless it should at least be considered a possibility. In fact for me to not mention it would be a severe dereliction of my duty as a human being. Having read some of the "hellish" accounts, and being familiar with warnings from various religions about the existence of hell, I want to do all in my power to stop a single soul experiencing such torment. I would rather include unpleasant truths in this book which cause it to be less popular, than ignore harsh realities to sell more copies. If I only sell one copy, but that copy results in someone being "saved" from an experience so traumatic the brain stops your memory recalling it, then all the effort I have put into this project will be worthwhile.

Suffice to say, with our current level of knowledge, it is not possible to say with any certainty that people who have a CA and don't report NDEs are unable to report them because they don't remember them—either because they cannot form spiritual or dreamlike memories or they simply struggle to remember in general or they are suffering from dissociative amnesia.

Any of these explanations is potentially valid.

But putting them aside for a moment, there is an elephant in the room when it comes to the issue of remembering NDEs, one that meant this section maybe should have been titled "Why would someone remember an

NDE". This points to the fact that not only does the brain have no ability to receive sensory information when someone is in a state of clinical death, but also it has no ability to remember it. If memory is a function of brain activity then no one should remember NDEs at all, so all these physiological reasons are but moot points.

2. WHY MIGHT THE CONSCIOUSNESS NOT DETACH FROM THE BRAIN?

The second possible explanation for the low incidence of NDEs—namely the 80 to 90% of CAs that do not result in one—is somewhat supported by the data from studies mentioned earlier, in which some patients who had more than one CA experienced only one NDE. Of course, it could be that, because of different procedures or circumstances involved in each of the CAs, their memory was affected to different degrees, but it could also be other reasons that are not obvious. Again, referring to the idea of spiritual aptitude, it may be that people who are more spiritual due to genetics, have a greater natural ability to "disconnect" their consciousness from their brains. If this ability is not an on/off ability, but rather exists as a spectrum, like most abilities, then it makes sense that some patients who have more than one CA on two different occasions, will have only one NDE.

To explain this, imagine someone who is a professional golfer of modest ability. On occasional days he may exceed his normal ability and win a tournament, but on most he will be placed in the middle of the field, whereas a golfer of high ability should consistently lead the field. For similar reasons it is possible to imagine that someone who is very "spiritual" will always have an NDE (or always remember it), whereas someone who is spiritually less sensitive may only experience or remember an NDE on rare occasions.

Which leads to another possible reason: the individual may be in a state between having an eternal soul and having a material-bound, dying soul. The eternal light of the soul may be flickering due to the lack of spiritual exercise or practise, but there may still be hope. Maybe this is why some people have auditory NDEs. Is it possible that the conscious has partly detached from the brain, but is somehow stuck in the physical location? This is all highly speculative, and somewhat imaginative though.

3. WHY WOULD SOMEONE'S CONSCIOUSNESS BE INCAPABLE OF PROGRESSING TO THE NEXT DIMENSION?

There is a third potential explanation for why only 10–20% of people who have a CA will report an NDE. Namely, at the time of their CA, their consciousness—from an eternal perspective—is dead or dying. It has become so entwined, so enamored with the physical dimension in the world surrounding us, that it is unable to escape this material dimension—or stronghold—it inhabits and eventually dies with it. It has been "materialized."

Another thought is that some people are born with only this type of material soul, which leads to the question: is it possible for some people to be born without an eternal soul? No. While I personally believe that most animals have a different level of consciousness to humans, I do not believe that having a fully functioning and potentially eternal soul is an accident of birth. All humans are born with the capacity to escape the physical dimension on dying and reach the "realms" or dimensions described and reported by countless NDErs—many of whom also had veridical OBEs.

This position is strongly supported by the unique evidence from childhood NDE reports. In general, there are fewer records of NDEs in children than in adults primarily because thankfully children are much less likely than adults to have a CA and be resuscitated. However, children do experience NDEs in ways that are very similar to adult NDEs. These children report an incredibly loving Being of Light, tunnels, heavenly dimensions, OBEs, and so on, but with one major exception:

preteen children rarely report experiencing a life review. I will discuss this difference in my next book; it is not important for this discussion. However, what is of particular relevance is the statistic that children who do have a CA and achieve ROSC are much more likely than adults to have an NDE. According to the book *Closer to the Light* by Dr. Melvyn Morse, which focuses on childhood NDEs from his years in pediatric medicine, about 80–90% of children who die and are resuscitated can recall some sort of NDE in contrast to only 10% of elderly adults, and this is supported by even more recent research.[33]

Why could this be? There is little in the literature to suggest that children are less likely to suffer neuronal injury as a result of CA and subsequent ROSC, nor is there a radical difference in the medications used post CA except perhaps for dosing, but this will be related to smaller body size and usually results in similar concentrations in the plasma or CNS. Genetically, there is no difference between children and adults, and other than the enhanced learning abilities of children, and that adults have a slight decline in memory function with age (up to 25% in healthy seniors), the child's brain has no additional powers or functions that explains a 70–80% difference in reports of NDEs. Studies show that by age seventy, the amount of information recalled thirty minutes after hearing a story once is about 75% of the amount remembered by an eighteen-year-old.[34] However, according to Alexandra Trelle they do remember the event occurring:[35]

33   The figure of 85% is cited by the International Association Of Near Death Studies (IANDS). Morse added further evidence in a later book: Morse M. Parting visions: a new scientific paradigm. In: Bailey LW,Yates J, eds. The near-death experience: a reader. New York and London: Routledge, 1996: 299–318.

34   PsychCorp. Wechsler Memory Scale-Fourth Edition (WMS-IV) Technical and Interpretative Manual. San Antonio, TX, Pearson, 2009.

35   Episodic Memory Decline in Healthy Ageing Alexandra Nicole Trelle Department of Psychology St John's College Dissertation for the degree of Doctor of Philosophy University of Cambridge May 2016.

Age-related changes in episodic memory are not "all-or-none" such that older adults simply cannot remember past experiences or recall fewer experiences than younger adults. Instead, aging is thought to affect the quality of one's memory, reducing the ability to recollect rich and detailed accounts of past experiences but leaving memory for more general aspects, or "the gist" of previous events relatively intact.[36] In particular, older adults tend to exhibit a decline in the ability to recover specific event details but display relatively intact memory for more general aspects of previous events.[37]

The results from a meta analysis of studies looking at changes in episodic memory with age, (specifically recollection and familiarity), showed a mean decline in recollection of 34% between young (age <30) and old (age >60), and a mean decline of 14% in familiarity[38]. Recollection is the ability to remember details or specifics of an event, and familiarity is the ability to remember that an event happened. Neither of these numbers is close to 80% and therefore cannot account for the huge disparity between incidence of NDE reports between the very young and the old.

An interesting piece of research[39] that looks at dream recall frequency showed similar declines over age, with young adults recalling about 10 dreams per month and the elderly 7 dreams per month. There was a marked

36   Levine, B., Svoboda, E., Hay, J., Winocur, G., & Moscovitch, M. (2002). Aging and autobiographical memory: Dissociating episodic from semantic retrieval. Psychology and Aging, 17, 677–689.

37   Craik, F.I.M. (1994). Memory changes in normal aging. Current Directions in Psychological Science, 3, 155–158; Schacter, Koutstaal, & Norman, 1997) Schacter, D.L., Koutstaal, W., & Norman, K.A. (1997). False memories and aging. Trends in Cognitive Sciences, 1, 229–236.

38   Koen and Yonelinas; Neuropsychol Rev. 2014 September ; 24(3): 332–354 .

39   Variations in Dream Recall Frequency and Dream Theme Diversity by Age and Sex; Tore Nielsen; Front Neurol. 2012; 3: 106

difference between males and females of all ages, with men having lower dream recall frequency than females, but still nothing like the difference observed between children and adults in NDE recall.

Another relevant piece of information is that the reduction in the number of reports of NDEs occurs gradually with age rather than an immediate "cliff edge" at the age of eighteen. Dr. Morse saw 85% NDEs in children, Ring noted 48% NDEs in a mean age of thirty-seven years, Sabom saw 43% NDEs in people with a mean age of 49 years, Van Lommel observed a rate of 12% having core experience with a mean age of 62 and in AWARE I 9% had NDEs with a mean age of 64; thus, age and the frequency of the experience seem to be associated.[40]

Again, these differences are not consistent with changes in memory over age. Then when you add the fact that a brain's memory forming ability is of no relevance when the brain is not functioning, we need to abandon the idea that impaired memory function - whether it be age related, or due to insult to the brain from drugs or procedures etc is behind this very significant discrepancy between elderly adults and children. So, if there is no physiological explanation, why do most children have NDEs and most adults over sixty years old don't? One possible answer is this idea of the materialization of the soul leading eventually to spiritual death when the host body dies.

My subjective understanding of God, and the accounts of the Being of Light, suggests that God is loving, generous, and wants to accept us. The idea that this grander Being could allow a human being to come into existence only to be condemned to endless suffering, is anathema to me. While it appears that some experiences seem like hell, we do not know that it is eternal, and I suspect—or rather hope— there may be an alternate, more merciful outcome: spiritual death. Is it possible that some souls, possibly even most souls, do not live beyond physical death, but rather than pass into

---

40   Van Lommel, P. THE LANCET • Vol 358 • December 15, 2001.

a dark or a hellish place they simply cease to exist? Maybe both happens. Maybe, as my prophet suggests, souls are indeed destroyed but not here on earth, but actually in Hell, a place NDErs claim exists and a place without light or hope where the flame of eternal life may eventually be extinguished by despair. I leave further discussions on this possibility, and the "fairness" of such an outcome, to my book *Did Jesus Die For Nothing?* We do not know for sure, but if we speculate that this explanation is accurate, then it is worth considering what might cause this materialization or death of the eternal soul after childhood.

AVOIDING SPIRITUAL DEATH

In a recent interview, Dr. Sam Parnia was asked what NDEs tell us about religion. His response was:

"As regards religion and even philosophy—of course, this is complex. Clearly throughout time and in every civilization, there have been some individuals who have proclaimed that our lives, actions, thoughts, and even intentions towards others are not meaningless and that we are not annihilated with death. Now for the first time in history, science is exploring death itself and what happens after death. What these experiences do provide is support for that line of thought. However, they do not support much of what else is associated with religion. For instance, people do not experience [exactly] what their religions had taught them, and atheists and agnostics also experience the same review of their lives and lucidity with death. So, in short, this experience and what science is discovering at the time of death seems to transcend any specific religious doctrine. These experiences also do not support much of the rest of what is associated with religion—i.e., specific rituals, sociocultural aspects, and so on."[41]

---

41   https://neo.life/2022/08/your-brain-at-the-moment-of-death/

On this subject I partly agree in that religion, as in man-made organisations with hierarchical structures, can be completely unrelated to God. However, if you regard religion as a set of teachings and example, given by a human being who claims knowledge of God, and that enhance our ability to access God and behave in the way he wants, then I totally disagree with Dr Parnia. I particularly disagree with his suggestion that the NDE transcends any specific religious doctrine. I will save the reasons for my believing that the gospels are not transcended by what we learn from NDEs for my book *Did Jesus Die For Nothing?* However, in my experience, while NDEs are very informative and compliment or enhance existing religious understanding, due to their diverse and often contradictory nature it is impossible to form a consistent set of teachings to guide us. Yes, we are taught we must love, but NDEs do not tell how us how to love, and equally importantly they do not tell us much about how not to behave to avoid potential spiritual death.

In some religions, followers are taught that "sin" causes—or leads to— death. In my understanding, most sin is a matter of exchanging the spiritual for the material. By this I mean compromising how God says we are to live and what we are to value versus how the world around us influences our behaviour. It means exchanging financial integrity for dishonest means of gain; loving sexuality for inappropriate or hedonistic acts of lust; friendship for power and high status; generosity and kindness for materialism and corruption; compassion for violence and dishonesty; good health and a happy home for gluttony and drunkenness; peace and joy for worry and envy. Most children have not had a chance to become deceived in this way— they are still developing.

Maybe what we are seeing with at least a portion of the 90% is that once some humans progress into adulthood and pursue the material dimension, their consciousness becomes so captivated by the temptations of this world that it has become, in essence, material and therefore unable to move to the heavenly dimension. It has either withered due to a lack of "spiritual nourishment," or, because of focus on things that are ultimately dead, the soul dies with the passing of the material world—it is not eternal.

In this scenario, death is not a punishment doled out by a vindictive God, but a natural consequence of ignoring all the people he sent to this dimension to show us how we should live in order to attain eternal life.

Given this, it is worth mentioning here what I have hinted at before: the future of our souls is in our hands, and our behavior determines whether or not our souls will survive death and find eternal peace and joy.

Many religions give guidance for how we should live and behave. I believe very strongly that my own faith is the way toward eternal life, but whether or not that is something you accept, the fact remains that many faiths have certain common themes consistent with the accounts of people who have met the Being of Light. These faiths focus on loving others as yourself; showing compassion and kindness; seeking knowledge, especially on spiritual matters; avoiding a focus on material wealth or power; avoiding competition at the expense of others' well-being. It means being generous and not killing others. These are good starting points for living a life which is encouraged by the accounts of those who have returned from death. My religion also provides hope for those who have perhaps done seemingly irreparable damage to their consciousness, maybe even to the point of appearing to materialize the eternal part of their souls, but I will save that discussion for *Did Jesus Die For Nothing?*

FINAL THOUGHTS

Before we leave this vitally important topic, I want to go right back to the beginning and the words of Dr Parnia in his discussion with Morgan Freeman:

"The evidence we have is that when we die the soul doesn't become annihilated."

We have come so far, haven't we? We now know that for some, at least, this appears to be true, but what Dr Parnia does not mention, nor any of his colleagues in the field, is that it may indeed be possible that in some instances the soul does become annihilated. All we ever seem to get from writers of books about NDEs is the good news, and while I believe it is important to maintain a positive perspective in life, if the truth is not all roses, it is important we know about potential threats to our well being rather than hide our heads in the sand.

So far I have tried hard to keep my own faith out of this book, but in relation to the last section, there is one particular verse from the New Testament that just keeps coming to mind, and is so absolutely in line with this very important topic that I feel compelled to include it:

"Enter through the narrow gate. For wide is the gate and broad is the road that leads to destruction, and many enter through it. But small is the gate and narrow the road that leads to life, and only a few find it." Matthew 7:13-14

I am not really that familiar with the teachings of other prophets, and it's possible that they say similar things. Whether or not they did, Jesus here is talking about eternal life, and he very clearly states that the majority will not get to see life beyond death. That now appears to be confirmed from our knowledge of NDEs. To be honest, before I became aware of the data from NDEs, despite my knowing these words, I didn't really take them that seriously. Like most other people, I assumed, or rather hoped, that everyone makes it in the end. However, if the fact that only ten percent of the elderly experience NDEs is not due to memory loss, or some genetic reason, then why is it? Is it that the longer we live, the more we are exposed to this materialistic life and make materialistic choices, the higher the chance that our souls become "materialised" and are destined to annihilation? Is it only a few who learn to live in such a way that they protect their souls from the material nature of the world?

As I said, the evidence on this is not straight forward, as seemingly un-spiritual people report NDEs. Whatever the truth on this issue is, understanding that there may be eternal consequences to our behavior in this life, could be one of the most important things anyone could learn. It is possible that by being made aware of this, people will change their approach to life to be more spiritual and love-focused. That may be the difference between life and destruction. I know that from my own personal experience, learning these things after studying the data about NDEs has really shaken me up, and taught me to take my faith much more seriously and make it my number one goal to follow God's commands, especially those that call me to be a more loving, compassionate person. I truly believe that nothing matters more, and that is why I have written this book.

SO, WHAT HAVE WE LEARNED?

- OBEs are proven to be real and the NDE is therefore very likely to be a real phenomenon as well.
- By inference, many of the core elements of the NDE are also likely to be real.
- A Being of Light—or God—exists. Many of us have known this all along, but the NDE gives us a much better evidence-based understanding of what this Being is like.
- Not everyone experiences pleasant encounters with lost relatives or the Being of Light—some have a hellish experience. This hellish experience may only be a temporary state.
- The majority of people who have a CA and achieve ROSC do not have an NDE. No one knows why. It could be due to memory, but there are other possible explanations. It makes sense that people need an eternal consciousness or soul that is able to leave the physical dimension to experience an NDE. Therefore, it is rational to speculate

that maybe some are unable to have an NDE because they don't have an eternal soul at the time of their CA and that the eternal part died—or is dying—in this life.

- Studies show that there is life after death for some of us or all of us. There includes a hellish experience for a minority, and for some, maybe even the majority, no experience at all—just the ending of existence. Others experience eternal access to the Being of Light, the space/time library, or other potentially very exciting possibilities, including the heavenly dimension.

There is little more to say, really, except that I ask you to consider deeply all that the data from NDEs and the AWARE studies mean. I believe they turn our materialistic world and our everyday perspectives upside down. It is now the right way up. If you understand the implications of the results, then you will focus more on how to improve your spiritual health. This is done by seeking knowledge about spiritual matters. By all means start by reading NDE accounts, but if you read enough you may begin to see, as I did, that there are too many inconsistencies and contradictions to conclude anything more specific than "be loving to each other". Yes, this is a wonderful way to live and *may* be enough, but when it comes to learning more about some of the deeper questions relating to the nature of our existence, and how to look after our souls, I believe it is vital to read what the founders of religions have to say. Once again though, it is important to note that despite what relativistic thinkers might claim, just as with NDE reports, there are mutually exclusive claims made by each key religious figure that force those who are seeking a path to make a choice as to which is right. I believe I have found the right path, and I explain the rationale for choosing that in *Did Jesus Die For Nothing*.

Whichever path you choose, I hope and pray that it will lead you to live a life of love that does not end with the death of your body, and will eventually result in an eternal relationship with the source of all life and love.

APPENDIX

MEMORY WHEN THERE IS NO BRAIN

NDErs' claims of having memory poses an interesting question: How can they remember if their brains aren't functioning, as proven by flatlining EEG? In other words, how can a completely shutdown brain lay down memory?

This opens up Pandora's box, so to speak. It has been assumed that memories are stored in the brain through the connection of neurons. If memories are stored somewhere other than the brain, where else are they stored? The answer to this may lie in two other aspects of NDEs that have been reported over the years.

First, people who report having a "life review" during an NDE report experiencing all the events of their life, and not just from their own perspective but from the perspective of those around them and those affected by their behavior. If a person's memories are stored only in his or her brain, this viewing from multiple perspectives would not be possible since these memories would die with the brain.

Second, as I mentioned before, some NDErs reported witnessing historical events from the perspective of participants in those events. Again, this would not be possible if the participants' memories of their existence were stored only in their individual brains. This perhaps suggests that all experience is stored "centrally" in some giant spiritual server—a library of all experience—and access is granted to anyone who has "passed over" to that dimension. In our modern times, we know that artificial memory can be stored electronically in computers, and that if you have the right computer and a good internet connection, you can access that memory from anywhere else in the world. In a dimension beyond our understanding, is it not therefore conceivable that all events could somehow be recorded in an analogous way?

I find this incredibly exciting, as I mentioned earlier. I love history and find it fascinating, and to know that I may be able to witness all human history—and maybe some non-human history too—thrills me beyond belief.

THE NATURE OF REALITY

My training in chemistry gives me a view of "matter" that shatters most peoples' perception of reality. When you look around, you may believe you are seeing solid objects, but the truth is, you are not. "Solidity" is an illusion created by the absorption of light by electrons orbiting atomic nuclei. Electrons and the protons in nuclei take up tiny amounts of space, but due to the nature of quantum mechanics and the speed of movement of sub-atomic particles, they create the appearance of solidity. Moreover, due to electrostatic repulsion when objects come into close proximity, objects "feel" solid. However, if all movement of electrons stopped, and all sub-atomic particles were brought into immediate juxtaposition, all objects—

such as trees and even buildings—would be invisible to the naked eye.[42]

Currently, I have a poor understanding of quantum mechanics, but from what I do understand, I sometimes feel nervous about the nature of "reality." I wonder, and I know others wonder as well, if it is in fact just a gigantic illusion.

How does this connect with the topic of NDEs? When I read about NDEs, some people describe their experiences of being in the spirit dimension as feeling more real than "real life" as we know it. Others refer to this life as a place of learning to prepare us for a next life. When you combine those subjective observations with the understanding of matter I just described, it does indeed make sense to understand the physical universe as illusory and our brains as the quantum processing machines allowing our consciousness to interface with this "illusion." There is a notion in quantum mechanics that a quantum state is not real until it is observed. Because we observe this illusion of reality through our consciousness, it lends the illusion a reality that it may not have had otherwise.

SOME WORDS FOR MY FELLOW CHRISTIANS

Some of you reading this may be Christians who are disturbed by my remarks and may even believe I am a heretic. I understand why you might arrive at this conclusion. Some of the ideas generated from the observations from NDEs are incompatible with biblical teaching, among others:

1. Reincarnation may occur.
2. Unbelievers don't suffer eternal hell.
3. Satan is never mentioned as a spiritual being.

---

42   To exemplify this point, it has been estimated that if you were to bring all the sub atomic particles that comprise the entire human race together it would be about the size of a sugar cube.

I discuss this in much greater detail in *Did Jesus Die For Nothing* which explores the relationship between Christian teachings and the findings from NDEs.

However, what I say to all Christians is that I go with what the facts tell us. I have absolute confidence in my understanding that God is real, that he created the universe and life, and that Jesus was God on Earth. The facts about NDEs as I observe them are completely compatible with this belief. I also believe that there is much more to support Christian beliefs that comes out of NDEs than there is to refute our faith. It provides convincing evidence for the existence of God as well as points to other aspects of our faith, such as the command to love being the most important one; that there is a heaven; there is also a hell; and we will face some kind of judgement. In fact, it is remarkable how much alignment exists between Christian doctrine and reports from NDEs.

However, on aspects of NDE testimony that conflict with Christian beliefs, we can settle on a position that is not in conflict. For instance, on the issue of reincarnation, which is rarely mentioned in historical NDEs, I would argue that it is not a helpful concept and a dangerous distraction, since the question of whether this existence is potentially the last for any given individual always remains. This makes the idea of having many lives a moot point and not worth arguing over, since the life we have now may be the only one that matters. Therefore, Christians ask the question, "Why take the chance you will get another life?" and embrace the wisdom to follow Jesus' teaching and do the best we can with the one life we have.

There are Christians who say that NDEs are satanic hallucinations, but I don't believe God would allow everyone—adults and children—who have completely separate experiences to be consistently lied to by Satan.

Christians need to resist dismissing science so readily and accept it when it makes the case for their beliefs. As more evidence emerges from the AWARE studies, curiosity about spirituality and the desire to explore faiths will skyrocket and atheists will have no answers. But we do. This is an amazing opportunity for the church.

THE CONUNDRUM OF HOW DNA AND LIFE CAME INTO BEING.

The central question posed in *DNA: The Elephant in the Lab* is whether scientific evidence points to life appearing as the result of a random process or whether life began due to intelligent initiation. If the latter, then there is evidence for the existence of some sort of super intelligent creator-type being, or God. I'm not talking about creationism or evolution, rather posing a question about where the science points to on the specific issue of the origin of life on earth. Going back to some of the original discussions around hypotheses, you have two competing mutually exclusive hypotheses, or statements:

1. Life came into being through a random natural process; or
2. Life was the result of an intelligent act.

As with all other hypotheses, they can be tested by assessing existing evidence or devising experiments to create evidence. The key problem is that the most basic forms of life—single-celled organisms such as bacteria—and the key processes that lie at the heart of life, specifically the translation of DNA into proteins, are in fact exceptionally complex. Yet these have been shown to exist in all known life forms since shortly after life on earth became possible. This presents an exceedingly difficult problem, and no one has come close to providing satisfactory theoretical routes by which life might have appeared. In other words, no one has provided credible evidence to support the first hypothesis.

According to mainstream media though, the question is all but answered. However, there is no scientific consensus except to state that because the modern scientific dogma of methodological materialism demands that everything we observe has a natural explanation, so, too, does the origin of life. The problem is that no one has explained how life began, even if you might be led to believe otherwise. For instance, if you google "origin of life" you'll find an article in Sciencemag, which is the web version of the highly respected magazine *Science*, which consolidates all the most important research from various fields in an intelligent and understandable format. This article has the title "Researchers may have solved origin-of-life conundrum."[43]

If a magazine such as *Science* is publishing this, then surely it is true! Or is it? …

Probe further, and when you read the researcher's original, in-depth review of the origin-of-life field in *Nature* you find a very different take on things. In the *Nature* article (the one cited in Sciencemag) Dr. John Sutherland, Professor of Chemistry at Cambridge University and one of the world's leading origin-of-life researchers, says:

Understanding how life on Earth might have originated is the major goal of origins of life chemistry. To proceed from simple feedstock molecules and energy sources to a living system requires extensive synthesis and coordinated assembly to occur over numerous steps, which are governed only by environmental factors and inherent chemical reactivity. Demonstrating such a process in the laboratory would show how life can start from the inanimate. If the starting materials were irrefutably primordial and the end result happened to bear an uncanny resemblance to extant biology—for what turned out to be purely chemical reasons, albeit elegantly subtle ones—then it could be a recapitulation of the way that natural life originated. We are not yet close to achieving this end, but recent results suggest that

43   https://www.sciencemag.org/news/2015/03/researchers-may-have-solved-origin-life-conundrum

we may have nearly finished the first phase: the beginning.[44]

Does that sound like Dr. Sutherland or any of his peers have solved the origin of life puzzle? He goes further and creates a graph, which I have simplified and adapted slightly to reflect how much progress has really been made.

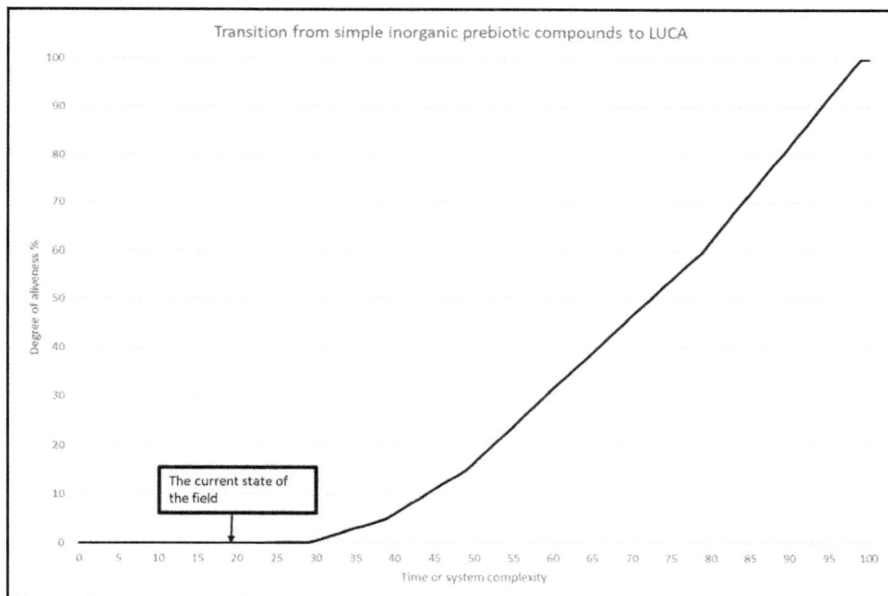

From Dr Sutherland's own view, we haven't even gotten to the starting line of understanding how life begins to develop complexity from the most basic molecules. (LUCA at the top right hand corner of the diagram is the Last Universal Common Ancestor, the cell from which all life is derived, and which science suggests lived around 3.7 billion years ago.)

So what's going on? Although scientists have had over fifty years since the elucidation of the DNA code, they have gotten precisely nowhere in determining how the DNA molecule itself, or the code, came into being, as

---

44   Studies on the origin Of Life—the end of the beginning; J.D. Sutherland; Nature Reviews Chemistry, Vol. 1:12 (2017).

Dr. Sutherland's graph elegantly demonstrates. The simple fact is that there is *no evidence at all* that life came into being through a random natural process. As well, there are no viable theories explaining the appearance of life—specifically the DNA-protein system—that lies at the heart of this life. The theories that have been touted, such as metabolism first or the RNA world theory, collapse under even the slightest scrutiny. In fact, there is a mountain of evidence against a natural origin of life.

I'll briefly discuss four examples here.[45]

1. For the first living system (a cell) to evolve or appear, large amounts of pure raw materials need to be available to form the DNA and/or proteins. These raw materials are nucleosides, the components of DNA, and amino acids, the components of proteins. To have successful reactions to create these raw materials, a host of conditions need to be set precisely. The idea that large amounts of pure nucleosides or amino acids would form together in an open environment in random conditions, is anathema to anyone who understands these processes. (Note: I am a PhD organic chemist who has worked with these specific chemicals, so I am reasonably well qualified to make that statement.) The idea that these nucleosides would then go on to form viable DNA (or RNA) molecules, or that amino acids would come together perfectly to form functional proteins, is beyond the realms of statistical probability in this universe.

    Dr. Sutherland claims he has found a path by which these raw materials could form in small quantities, but he does this in a laboratory under controlled conditions using pure starting materials. Could this same path occur naturally on a messy, newly formed earth? Although unlikely, I suspect it is possible, but from humans'

---

45   For a much more extensive analysis of this problem, please read my book *DNA: The Elephant in the Lab*, available at most online bookstores as an eBook or paperback.

knowledge of chemistry, the results would have been small amounts of impure substances that would not be of any use for the assembly of chains of DNA, RNA, or proteins. But even if by some extraordinary miracle, large amounts of pure nucleosides and amino acids formed spontaneously under the prevailing natural conditions, there would be much bigger obstacles that can't be overcome.

Firstly, to create the first living system (cell), a cell wall or membrane is needed to enclose and protect the new system, otherwise the components would just float off and not work together. Without this enclosure, life could not form. However, no one has proposed a viable route as to how this would happen.

Could the first systems have begun in cell-like structures within porous rocks or in oily bubbles spontaneously forming around these proto systems, as some suggest? Putting all the statistical issues aside, there is a big conceptual barrier to this proposition. The cell membrane is written into the DNA code of the cell. Having an external uncoded barrier, such as an oily bubble, does not explain how the code for a membrane eventually appears in the DNA. No one provides a viable explanation. In fact, evolutionary principles would work against the addition of such a code by random processes since there is no advantage to creating a new barrier, and yet without this segment of code, the system is forever trapped in the bubble or rock cell. It is a catch-22 and inconceivable how this cell wall problem might be overcome by natural processes, as evidenced by the fact that no one has conceived of a realistic solution.

2. The second big problem to overcome is the "numbers" problem. The myriad complex processes that occur in every living organism are the result of millions of proteins, often working in concert. Many proteins are like tiny nano-machines that perform very precise functions. They are central to life and have existed at least since our Last Universal

Common Ancestor (LUCA), which is a cell with the same biochemical foundations as modern life that existed about 3.7 billion years ago— not that long after the earth would have been able to support life for the first time. From this cell, life branched into the three domains: eukaryotes, archaea, and bacteria. Therefore, at some point, proteins needed to come into existence by a natural process. In nature, any proteins that might be produced outside of living systems would be generated randomly, either by some protein producing molecule, or by prevailing environmental conditions. The vast majority of random sequences of amino acids (the components of proteins) are completely useless. In fact, Seth Lloyd, an academic from MIT, calculated that the probability of producing a functional protein when assembling a chain of 150 amino acids in a random sequence was 1 in 1×10^{164}. This number is astronomically huge.

Some might say that everything is theoretically possible, but how likely is this? An elegant illustration of just how unlikely this probability has of occurring is shown in the book *Evolution: Possible or Impossible?* by James F. Coppedge.[46]

In an incredibly generous scenario, Coppedge writes that the entire earth is covered in a sea of amino acids; every oxygen, nitrogen, and carbon atom is used to form chains of amino acids which reform every second from the beginning of Earth's history until the present day. Even then, there is a vanishingly small chance that a functional protein will form. The author estimates how long it would take to generate one single functional protein, and the number is huge—well beyond the age of the universe.

To show the vastness of this number, even in the context of this protein factory Earth, the author illustrated another concurrent

---

46   A great write-up and video demonstrating the impossibility of this can be found at www.originthefilm/mathematics.php.

scenario in which an amoeba carries atoms across the known universe—which is billions of light years wide—while our amino acid Earth is producing proteins. Even if the amoeba moved every single atom in the universe across the universe, one atom at a time at a rate of one foot per year, this fictional earth covered in amino acids would not have had sufficient time to produce a functional protein. In fact, the amoeba would have to repeat the process of moving the universe one atom at a time, many billions of times before the amino acid-covered Earth had a reasonable chance of producing a single functional protein.

In reality Earth is not, and never was, a giant lake composed of amino acids. Even the likelihood of a small puddle of amino acids ever having existed through random natural processes is ridiculously small. As a result, it is in fact regarded by mathematicians as statistically impossible for a protein to form by chance alone. And the simplest cells have at least three hundred proteins! No one has proposed a solution to this unavoidable problem. Evolution does not solve this since you still have to randomly assemble proteins or proto proteins at some point, with the same statistical odds against that happening. This is significant evidence against life appearing through a random natural process.

3. The third example of evidence against a natural origin of life is the chicken and egg paradox that lies at the heart of the origin-of-life puzzle.

    DNA is a code for proteins, and proteins do all the work of life, including translating the DNA molecules into proteins.[47] The paradox is that the proteins could not come into existence without the DNA

---

47   Highschool biology textbooks state that translation is performed by the ribosome, which is a mixture of proteins and RNA molecules, but in fact, translation occurs in the cytoplasm when ARS proteins pair tRNA with the amino acid. Proteins do the translation, and there is no evidence of any alternative mechanism. This is discussed in a chapter all of its own in *DNA: The Elephant in The Lab*.

code, and yet without the proteins to translate them, the code would be meaningless and remain untranslated.

Some suggest the RNA world might be an intermediary world between the chemical building-block stage and the current DNA-protein-based world that we have today. However, the RNA world provides absolutely no explanation for the paradox. Most serious scientists who are familiar with this problem have long since abandoned any pretense that the RNA world offers a solution. I discuss this in detail in my book on the origin of DNA and describe it as a red herring. For those who really love science, I also discuss a rabbit hole inside the red herring!

The DNA code has both abstract and arbitrary qualities that are unique to codes and language. There are no other natural examples and there is no explanation as to how the DNA code and its translation apparatus could have formed through random natural processes. The creation of codes is unique to human ingenuity and requires intelligent thought to generate. Since it appears that preexisting external knowledge of the code would be required to assemble a storage and translation system, there is no viable way of conceiving how random natural processes, with no foresight or preexisting knowledge, could have been responsible for this incredible paradox. The evidence for this is that no one has conceived how this could happen. Some of the greatest minds in the world—such as Francis Crick, the co-discoverer of DNA—have pondered it. He concluded it came from outer space, but that only moves the problem somewhere else, and our universe is not big enough for a natural solution to this problem.

4. The fourth example of evidence against a natural origin of life is the frozen accident. Scientists have shown that life branched into different animal kingdoms from the Last Universal Common Ancestor (LUCA), which I mentioned earlier. There may have been some

gene swapping and transfers between the different domains early on; however, the one element that remained almost completely constant from LUCA through all its trillions of descendants was the DNA code and its translation system. The DNA code has not adapted, grown, or evolved—it has been frozen. The term "frozen accident" was coined to reflect the belief that the code evolved quickly and then froze in its current form, as it was perfect.

But that is not the most logical explanation of why the DNA code is frozen.

The translation of DNA involves the deployment of a large number of proteins and RNA molecules all working together in concert. The code changing in even the smallest manner—for example the addition of a new amino acid—would require multiple changes across many different molecules in one cell replication cycle. It is completely inconceivable that such a copious amount of changes could occur fortuitously and simultaneously in one step—as they would need to. Moreover, the molecules would need to have foresight of how the new code worked, and evolution does not have foresight. The statistical problems against the appearance of a protein by random processes—shown to be impossible earlier—seems trivial in comparison to the notion that the DNA code developed by a series of random processes.

Ultimately, the DNA code could not have evolved from something else because one simple step up from a smaller code would require an exceptionally large amount of changes to a similarly complex system.

Could the DNA code have evolved to this perfect point by accident? There is no evidence to support this possibility, and the evidence against this happening is overwhelming. Again, no one has pretended to explain this in a viable way.

In summary, when you look at the totality of scientific evidence regarding the hypothesis that life—in particular, DNA and its translation system—appeared through a random natural process, it is clear the balance of evidence is entirely against such an event. There is no evidence and no viable theories supporting the hypothesis, but rather a mountain of evidence *against* it happening. When taking an objective view of the scientific aspects, the hypothesis that life was the result of a random process is essentially all but proven wrong.

In the absence of an alternative hypothesis, it still cannot be completely discounted, but there is one—our second hypothesis—namely that life was the result of an intelligent act. Is there measurable evidence for or against this hypothesis?

EVIDENCE OF INTELLIGENCE

There are over a million codes that we know of—human codes, such as the human language, computer codes such as C++, and animal codes such as birdsongs or dog barks—that biologists have determined to have meaning to the animals involved. All of these codes have one thing in common: they were generated by an intelligent organism. No codes discovered to date have been the result of random natural chemical processes. We may observe natural complexity—such as the structure of a crystal produced due to chemical interactions—but not natural codes.

It has been established by information theorists, including Hubert Yokey—who was one of the world's leading bioinformatics experts—that the DNA code is not *like* a code, it actually *is* a code with both abstract and arbitrary properties that random chemical processes would be unable to produce.

Because all codes that we know of are the result of intelligence and DNA is a code, it is logical to conclude that the DNA code was most likely the result of intelligence. This conclusion is reinforced by the fact that there is no alternative viable explanation for its appearance. Random chemical evolutionary processes have been shown to be incapable of producing any of the key components of the simplest cells, let alone the remarkable molecule, DNA.

So, the answer to the question of whether there is other scientific evidence that a God exists, besides the reports from NDEs, is yes.

BIBLIOGRAPHY AND SELECTED WEB REFERENCES FOR FURTHER READING:

After by Bruce Greyson

Erasing Death by Dr. Sam Parnia and Josh Young

Life After Life by Raymond Moody

The Handbook of Near-Death Experiences: Thirty Years of Investigation by Janice Holden and Bruce Greyson

Lessons from the Light by Dr. Kenneth Ring and Evelyn Valarino

Light and Death: One Doctor's Fascinating Account of Near-Death Experiences by Michael Sabom

Near-Death Studies: An Overview by Kenneth Ring

Paranormal Experience and Survival of Death by Carl B. Becker

Consciousness Beyond Life: The Science of the Near-Death Experience by Pim van Lommel

Where God Lives: The Science of the Paranormal and How Our Brains are Linked to the Universe by Melvin Morse and Paul Perry

Closer to the Light: Learning from the Near-Death Experiences of Children by Melvin Morse and Paul Perry

God at the Speed of Light by Lee Baumann

Science and the Near-Death Experience: How Consciousness Survives Death by Chris Carter

My Descent into Death by Howard Storm

Evidence of The Afterlife by Jeffrey Long and Paul Perry

Near Death Research Foundation. http://www.nderf.org

International Association of Near-Death Studies. https://iands.org/home.html

Horizon Research Foundation. http://horizonresearch.org

Near-Death Experiences and the Afterlife. http://www.near-death.com

NYU Grossman School of Medicine/Parnia Lab. https://med.nyu.edu/research/parnia-lab

AwareofAware. https://awareofaware.co

ABOUT THE AUTHOR

Born in 1968 and now living in Sussex, England, I have spent my career in science. My undergraduate studies were in chemistry, and my PhD studies were in organic medicinal chemistry, during which I worked in a team that created a molecule that opened the door to a cure for Hepatitis C, as well as treatments for certain cancers, and HIV. In 1999, I began working in the pharmaceutical industry, for the first ten years helping to bring new drugs to market, and for the past ten years working alongside academic clinical investigators in designing, conducting, helping publish and interpreting clinical studies looking into the effects of exciting new compounds in diseases such as HIV, hematological malignancies, obesity, and, most recently, neurological disorders such as narcolepsy and Alzheimer's.

As a medical scientist, I have become skilled in understanding, interpreting, and disseminating key findings from complex clinical studies, similar in some ways to the AWARE studies. It is a part of my day job to be able to critique scientific data and understand how design can affect outcomes, among other things.

I also write a blog—awareofaware.com—exploring research into NDEs, which follows closely any developments in the AWARE studies. My blog focuses on the clinical data and the science. I also discuss possible "spiritual" implications that come out of the scientific research.

In addition, I am the author of *DNA: The Elephant in the Lab*, a non-fiction book about the origin of life, and I also wrote the novel *Deadly Medicine*. Both are available in online bookstores.

OTHER BOOKS BY ORSON WEDGWOOD:

Fiction
Deadly Medicine
Unholy Spirit: Part 1

Non-fiction
DNA: The Elephant In The Lab
Did Jesus Die For Nothing: The evidence from Near Death Experiences

www.ingramcontent.com/pod-product-compliance
Ingram Content Group UK Ltd.
Pitfield, Milton Keynes, MK11 3LW, UK
UKHW021354031125
8734UKWH00034B/1269

9 781838 363116